BIBLICAL ARCHAEOLOGY

IS VOLUME

62

OF THE

Twentieth Century Encyclopedia of Catholicism

UNDER SECTION

VI

THE WORD OF GOD

IT IS ALSO THE

55TH

VOLUME IN ORDER OF PUBLICATION

Edited by HENRI DANIEL-ROPS *of the Académie Française*

BIBLICAL ARCHAEOLOGY

By M. DU BUIT, O.P.

Translated from the French by KATHLEEN POND

HAWTHORN BOOKS · PUBLISHERS · *New York*

First Edition, December, 1960

NIHIL OBSTAT

Joannes M. T. Barton, S.T.D., L.S.S.

Censor Deputatus

IMPRIMATUR

E. Morrogh Bernard

Vicarius Generalis

Westmonasterii, die XXLV SEPTEMBRIS MCMLX

CONTENTS

INTRODUCTION

The principle of archaeological method is a direct result of the natural process of the accumulation of ruins. It is a well-known fact that the soil of towns is constantly rising, as may easily be observed in the old quarters of our own cities. Whether we are preserving buildings or reconstructing them, we never take away as much material as we bring to them. At the time when houses of unbaked brick were frequently collapsing, people did not take the trouble to clear the ground for reconstruction, but were satisfied with levelling it. When a war happened to destroy the town and cause it to be abandoned, the wind carried the dust right on top of the walls. Thus the artificial hill or "tell" was gradually formed. It was generally easy to recognize by its flat top and its regular slopes.

In these circumstances the method of the archaeologist is patiently to undo what history and nature have brought about. The tell is excavated and a most careful record made of all that is discovered and will soon have to be destroyed: the uppermost remains are the most recent, those found deep down the most ancient; thus at the same time as objects are discovered, their chronological sequence is ascertained.

If the principle is simple, its application is much less so: the natural slope of the ground, high walls standing one on top of the other, terrace-work constructed by ancient inhabitants, are sufficient to introduce in practice numerous complications, into the detail of which we need not enter. The best clue to unravel such difficulties is provided by pottery. The ancients used pottery to a very considerable extent, and there is no place where it is not possible to find at least some shards. Systematic investigation has shown that as regards technique, quality of the clay and shape, each period had its own styles and processes. If we begin, then, with sites where the stratification is clear, and whose history is well known from other sources, we can determine the evolution of pottery styles, and can then unravel more complicated layers and determine dates in cases in which the literary documents are silent.

The paradox of archaeology is that for it peace destroys and war preserves. An attack and a fire leave walls standing upon some height and a quantity of objects on the ground, broken, it is true, but such as a good craftsman will be able to reconstruct; if a few centuries of neglect come and seal all of it off under a thick layer of earth, first-class archaeological strata will be the result. In a time of peace, on the other hand, the buildings are cared for and may last through many generations, in which continual rebuilding will complicate the original plans, perhaps to the point of making them undiscoverable; the debris is cleaned up, the materials used again, the soil rises slowly and strata very remote from each other in point of time are scarcely distinguishable on the site and contain only a small number of recognizable objects. That is why very little remains of the ancient and brilliant civilization of Tyre and Sidon: their unbroken activity until well into the Middle Ages has constantly effaced the traces of the past, the site of Tyre is still occupied by a small town, and had it not been for the intervention of the Lebanese administration the tell of Sidon would today be covered with new houses. In that case one is reduced to excavating the necropoli which in ancient times were often pillaged and which in any case only provide limited material. On the other hand, ancient Ugarit (Ras-Shamra), destroyed about 1200 B.C. by "the Peoples of the Sea" and never rebuilt since, has provided the easily decipherable traces of a large city with quantities of the richest material: pottery, bronzes, ivories, inscribed tablets. The same is the case with several sites in the interior of Syria —these cities on the borders of the desert were brought to prosperity by successive empires, and when these empires were destroyed one after the other, the cities were abandoned.

The whole of archaeology, moreover, is an adventure, and there is often found in it something other than what was sought. For instance, in Jericho, no trace has been found of the walls overthrown by Josue, but unsuspected neolithic civilizations have been discovered. It is doubtless this sort of thing that explains the intense keenness of genuine excavators.

A manual or a methodical introduction should give many other details on these questions. It should also indicate what the principal excavations in Palestine have been, what progress they have brought to method, what were the external features of the results and how the chronology has become increasingly accurate. But we are interested in practical conclusions, so we shall confine ourselves to a selection of the best authenticated results, showing how these illustrate the life and customs of the ancient people of Israel.

Similarly, no attempt will be made to deal with the pre-history and proto-history of Palestine, despite their very great interest. It will be sufficient to indicate that the Jericho excavations have recently shown the existence of an authentic neolithic city, well built and fortified as early as the eighth millennium before our era, the economy of which must have been based on the cultivation of crops for which irrigation was provided by the neighbouring oasis. It was at the beginning of the third millennium that the use of metals, writing and the organization of great states developed simultaneously. The Hebrew patriarchs, therefore, coming a thousand years or more later were late-comers in the history of civilization. It will be sufficient for our purpose, however, to begin this study in actual fact with the Canaanites of the second millennium, the men against whom the people of Israel had to fight and from whom they borrowed part of their civilization.

Finally, no attempt will be made to present here all that a century of research has made known to us of the Egyptian, Assyrian, Babylonian and Persian empires, despite the many allusions to them in the Bible. Such results, moreover, are fairly well known to the public. On the other hand, we shall endeavour in this book only to have recourse to Palestinian or at least to Syro-Phoenician material, material which is in general less known, the original character of which deserves to be brought into prominence.

CHAPTER I

POTTERY

As has already been indicated, the detailed examination of pottery is the best clue for establishing the chronology of an excavation site. It is also a good means of getting to know the development of material life in its humble and day-to-day aspects. Changes of style witness to the arrival of new influences and perhaps of new populations, technical quality reflects prosperity and taste, and certain degrees of progress have had their practical importance. It is rather from this point of view that we should now like to describe the evolution of Palestinian pottery.

TECHNIQUE

In the first place, however, a few remarks must be made about technique. The potter's art has not perceptibly evolved since the beginning of the second millennium, and present-day artisans still work with the same tools and the same methods. As a type of the workshop of ancient times we may take that of the Essenes of Qumrân, one of the best preserved still left to us (fig. 1). A carefully cemented shallow trench was used to tread the clay in order to eliminate the impurities (*a*); by the side of this was a small basin containing the necessary water reserve (*b*). Once prepared and formed into balls, the clay lay in another deeper trench (*c*). The wheel was installed in a round pit (*d*). The potter sitting on the edge worked the lower plate with his feet and worked the piece placed on the upper plate (*e*) with his hands. The purpose of these movements was to give the piece a regular shape and at the same time to give a foliated structure to the clay which increases its resistance. The piece, after brief drying in the air, was finally baked in an oven. At Qumrân, an oven for the large pieces of pottery had a receptacle for the fire below and, half-way up, a ledge on which the pieces were laid, accessible from outside (f). In another, smaller oven, the fire receptacle was covered with a shelf pierced with holes on which the pieces were laid. In both cases the oven was covered with a dome pierced by a smoke vent.

FIG. 1. THE POTTER'S WORK
Plan after *Revue Biblique*, 1956

MIDDLE BRONZE II

Brought to perfection at the beginning of the period with which we are concerned, this technique quickly produced shapes of a beauty unknown until that time. After a short transition period, the era which it has been agreed to call Middle Bronze II has left us pottery which it is easy to recognize: the clay is fine in quality, grey in colour in the ordinary pieces, pink or beige in the better ones. Despite a considerable variety the types have a certain air of similarity: ovoid body with pointed base, neck funnel-shaped and somewhat long, a small foot often on a tripod (fig. 3, 25), large handles elegantly curved, carefully moulded details. Decoration is rare. Among the most usual forms the following should be noted: fig. 2: small jars 32, 40, 41, jugs with trefoil opening 42, pitchers with pointed lip 43, footed vases varying in depth 44, bowls and dishes of a simple or complex curve 37, 38, 45, 46; fig. 3: jars with or without handles 21, 22, 23, large pots 25, pitchers 26.

There are no foreign importations; on the contrary, Middle Bronze pottery from Palestine has been found in the Nile delta at levels corresponding to the Hyksos domination, thus fixing the duration of this period between the twentieth and the sixteenth centuries.

LATE BRONZE

The isolation of Syria and Palestine was then broken by the expansion of the new Egyptian empire and its rivals, the Mitanian empire of Upper Mesopotamia and then the Hittite of Anatolia. At the same time maritime relations were established with the islands of the Aegean Sea. The new civilization received the name of Late Bronze. Although the backwash of politics brought numerous destructions in its wake, the development of commerce can be recognized by the massive importations of foreign pottery, which was usually painted. Side by side with these can be distinguished the more or less successful local imitations, usually easy to identify.

This influence, however, did not extend beyond the plains bordering the coast, and few foreign forms penetrated to the mountains of the interior in any quantity. Among them may be instanced miniatures *pyxides* and *askoi* (fig. 2, 35, 36, though a genuine pyxide should be flat-bottomed), or again "pilgrims' gourds" (fig. 3, 27—a particularly well-made model, with small handles—"flaps"—through which a string could be threaded and the neck extended into a cup).

The native tradition, nevertheless, remained very much alive everywhere and almost all the Middle Bronze forms were found during the Late Bronze era. It is true that the clay is not quite of the same quality and the curve a little stiff, but these are only small points.

Some cases do, however, show real decadence (fig. 2: pitcher *33* with its shortened handle and the small and badly shaped pitcher *26*). There are also new features which prelude the following period (fig. 2: pitcher *31,* somewhat heavy, small jug with handle *34,* pitcher with round bottom *25*; fig. 3: large

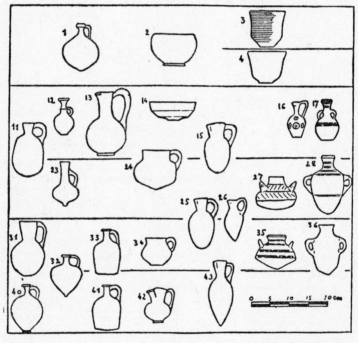

FIG. 2. POTTERY.

pitcher *20* and, in particular, the cooking-pot for the fire *24*, the invention of which must have considerably modified practical life).

IRON AGE I

The Late Bronze strata are generally broken into by brutal destructions, and covered over by strata known as "Iron Age I", for it was then that this metal was first found in appreciable quantities. It has been generally agreed that such destructions should be related to the invasions which caused such havoc in the Orient at the beginning of the twelfth century: the

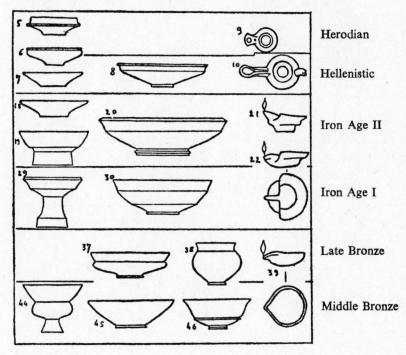

Herodian

Hellenistic

Iron Age II

Iron Age I

Late Bronze

Middle Bronze

SMALL PIECES

Peoples of the Sea on the coast, Arameans and Israelites in the interior. The lower standard of technique is striking: the clay is coarse, grey, brown or brick-red in colour; the pieces are heavy and without any external finish: the curved shapes are replaced by carinated forms with a polygonal outline (fig. 2, *29, 30*); necks and feet disappear or are negligently formed, handles are multiplied but no longer have any decorative value (fig. 3, *16, 18*).

The majority of the shapes, however, are derived from the previous period (fig. 2, small pitcher *11*, jar *24*, pitchers *25* and *26*, footed vase *29*, dish *30*, lamp *22*, fig. 3: large jars *16* and *17*, cooking pot *19*). Even certain foreign forms are maintained (fig. 2, *27, 28*). A new feature is the small pitcher with handle attached to the middle of the neck (fig. 2, *23*). Thus the newcomers have brought with them scarcely anything and did not succeed in preserving what was best in the tradition of their predecessors.

On the coastal plain the tradition of painted pottery was maintained, and the different foreign styles formed a composite that was somewhat heavy and characterless but not altogether devoid of the picturesque. To this the name of "Philistine pottery" was given, although the Philistines were not the inventors of it.

IRON AGE II

The pottery of Iron Age I gradually developed in the direction of a new type which came into prominence in the second half of the era of the kings of Israel and Juda, Iron Age II. While it is not of high quality the clay is better than in the preceding period. The surface of the most carefully finished pieces is often decorated by lines obtained by polishing with a small pebble or with a shell. This last method, however, seems to have developed principally in Juda and other examples exist of slight differences between the two Israelite kingdoms.

The forms often show careful work (cf. in fig. 2 dishes *20* and *30*, pitchers *12* and *23*, on fig. 3 cooking pots *13* and *19*); it may even happen that an excess of work spoils the appearance of a piece (fig. 3, *14*). The ovoid types have disappeared, cylindrical types have become general, ventricose forms of the base occur (fig. 3, *10, 11, 12, 14*). Drinking pots seem in the process of being replaced by simple bowls (fig. 2, *14*), and footed vases by plates (fig. 2, *18, 19*). Lamps are mounted on small feet (fig. 2, *21*). Again small jugs of pretty red clay decorated with bands and circles painted black (fig. 2, *16, 17*) were imported from Cyprus (or Tyre?), and it is doubtless to foreign imitation that must be attributed the pottery of fine yellow clay decorated with red painting and with an elegant curve which is chiefly found in Samaria and the neighbourhood (fig. 2, *13*). In the uppermost strata of this period, one often finds a few pieces of tableware that was known at Nineveh, and was used by the Assyrian garrisons.

HELLENISTIC POTTERY

The era of the Persian and Macedonian empires has not left us sufficient series of pottery for it to be possible to follow the evolution which took place at that time. The clearest evidence is provided by the imported pieces: Attic ceramic under the Persians, then large wine amphorae from Rhodes under the Macedonians. This evolution led to a fixed type of appearance found in the ruins of Bethsur (Bethoron 164–140 B.C., cf. I Mach. 4. 29, etc.), and again in the deepest stratum of Qumrân (100–31 B.C.): the Hellenistic type.

Certain forms inherited from the Iron Age can be recognized (fig. 3: compare *1, 2, 3* with *10, 11 12*; fig. 2, compare *7* and *18*). But the cooking pots have a narrow neck (fig. 3, *5*), the pitchers are entirely new (fig. 2, *1* and fig. 3, *8*), as are also the bowls, goblets, lids and lamps (fig. 3, *7*, fig. 2, *2, 4, 10*). The "pilgrims' gourds" are still made of two halves stuck together but they are inflated to the point of losing that

Herodian

Hellenistic

Iron Age II

Iron Age I

Late Bronze

Middle Bronze

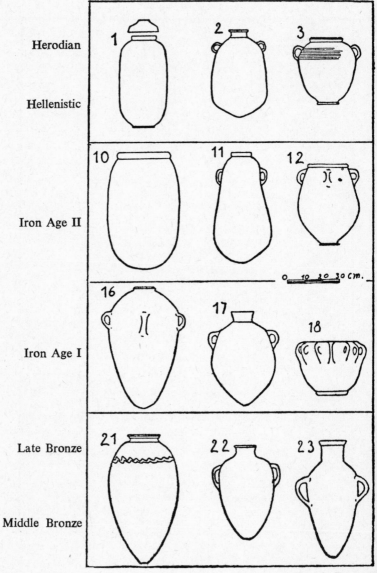

FIG. 3. POTTERY

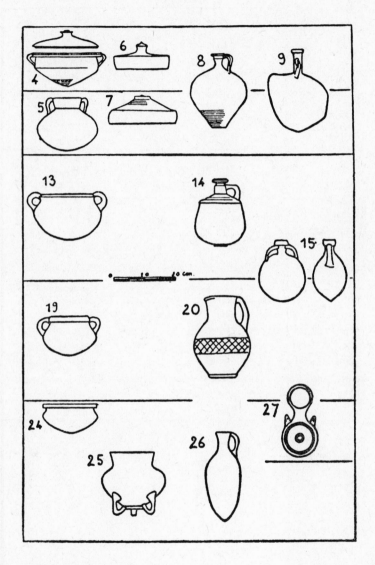

Large Pieces

flattened form which was their original *raison d'être* (fig. 3, 9). The clay is finer than in the Iron Ages, the pieces less heavy, but appearance is neglected, the colour lustreless, the curve mediocre. This pottery does not give the impression of lack of technical skill, but rather of an absence of interest due to the fact that the pursuit of elegance was turned in other directions.

HERODIAN POTTERY

The Khirbet Qumrân has provided a second stratum (4 B.C.–A.D. 68) in which a perceptible development can be seen. Since this is also found in the Herodian palace in Jericho and in tombs dated by coins, it is convenient to name it "Herodian", as is often done.

Again forms have become more sharply defined, often accentuated by a fillet (fig. 3, compare lids 6 and 7), and it is not always an advantage (fig. 2, plates 5 and 6). More and more do we find surfaces decorated with fine ribs made on the potter's wheel (fig. 2, goblets 3 and 4). Now that the way to make conveniently wide lids has been learnt, a return is made to cooking pots with a large opening (fig. 3, 4), while at the same time the earlier type continues to follow the general evolution. On the other hand lamps become smaller and simpler (fig. 2, 9 and 10); the small Herodian lamp is very characteristic of this period. All these tendencies are further accentuated under the Roman and Byzantine empires. They show well enough the approach of the ordinary people to a kind of humble elegance consisting of care and neatness.

CHAPTER II

CITIES IN THE ISRAELITE PERIOD

FORTIFICATION

In architecture as in pottery, almost the only result of Israel's contact with the Canaanite inheritance in Iron Age I was to impoverish it.

So far as fortifications were concerned, people were satisfied with maintaining those already erected (figs. 4 and 5). In places where the slope of a hill provided no natural defence, this was supplied by first of all raising a thick bank of earth (*a*) on which the wall proper was constructed, of unbaked bricks on a foundation of stones (*b*); here and there a wider foundation points to the presence of a tower (*c*) and we know from the Egyptian pictures that it was crowned with a wooden transom. A door was cut in a massive tower where the passage was narrowed by two or three embrasures closed by shutters during the night or in time of war (*d*), a ramp or stairway led up to it from the foot of the hill and its top was sometimes surmounted by an

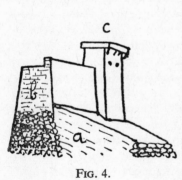

Fig. 4.

outwork (f), a device rare in the Late Bronze age but which became general later.

Towards the beginning of the time of the Kings, we frequently find the wall lined by a row of long, narrow casemates whose purpose was apparently to maintain a continuous encircling road for the houses were built leaning against the wall (fig. 9, Tell Beit Mirsim; here the entrance consisted of a simple mound supporting a tower, and of a zigzag passage).

ARCHITECTURE

Inside the towns streets and sewers, although known to the Canaanites, have disappeared (fig. 5). The houses are small dwellings grouped around a courtyard, a system necessitated by the country's poverty in timber and inherited from the Canaanites, but the actual workmanship is, generally speaking, less satisfactory. Thus, progress through the city was only possible by going round from one courtyard to another. The agglomeration of the houses probably corresponded to the grouping of families round the patriarch or the senior heads of families. This system was of rural origin, and when adapted to urban life the individual units seem to have developed haphazard until the whole of the unoccupied space was filled.

At Tell el Far'ah, ancient Tirza, an erection with a raised stone and a small basin (fig. 5, g) was found opposite the door. There were large houses with a fairly clear arrangement—an entrance courtyard surrounded by rooms and huts on pillars (h); other buildings are more modest and on the whole the evidence suggests that these were more numerous (j); others again seem to follow no particular plan (k); a kind of "private road" (l) joins a large house and two smaller ones.

Fortification improved in the time of the Kings. Under Solomon the northern gate of Megiddo brought the Canaanite system to a degree of strength never before achieved (fig. 8, h); the corresponding wall, however, is made of a series of elements which either project or are slightly in recess, the purpose of which is obscure; it does not include towers. The latter made their appearance towards the year 900 in the wall of Mizpa; the fact that they were at most fifty-four yards apart allowed of regular flanking (fig. 7).

Once achieved, this system became general. It has been found among others at Megiddo in the strata pertaining to Jehu's dynasty. The recesses of Solomon's wall were blocked up on the inside and the alternate salients were enlarged to serve as a basis for a tower. The gateway was simplified (fig. 8 a).

After the havoc and destruction of the Aramean wars, the period of Jeroboam II in Israel and Osias in Juda has left distinct strata typical of Iron Age II, in various places. Streets reappear, sometimes constructed to a plan as at Tirza (fig. 6), sometimes traced along the natural lines of the hill as at Tell Beit Mirsim (fig. 9). Sewers have also been discovered as at Tell Beit Mirsim (c) or at Megiddo (g) and elsewhere. A "palace" or administrative building is frequently to be found near the principal gate, as at Megiddo (b, c) or Mizpa (b).

At Tirza, where it has been possible to make a better reconstruction of the details of the plan, the traditional stele and its basin were situated near the door (fig. 6, a). The "palace" has both an external courtyard (b) and an internal courtyard (c) surrounded by living and reception rooms or by shops. One group of planned buildings (d) is in very poor condition. It is separated by a street (e) from another group where two houses (h) can be identified whose type derives from the previous period, though the workmanship is more skilled. An alley separates these from a group of houses (j) in the worst native tradition. Similarly at Tell Beit Mirsim, the streets separate blocks of houses from courtyards and small dwellings. The new features had had no impact on the mass of the population.

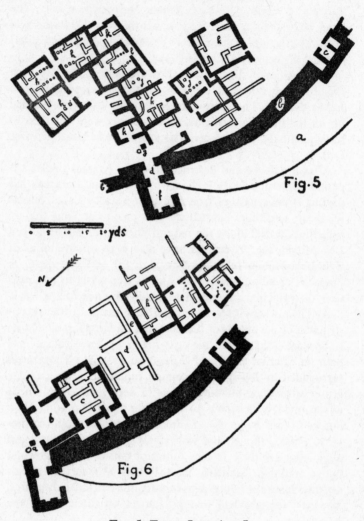

FIG. 5. TIRZA. IRON AGE I
FIG. 6. TIRZA. IRON AGE II
Plans after *Revue Biblique* 1951-1955

ROYAL BUILDINGS

The royal buildings must be dealt with separately. The most remarkable are those of the citadel of Samaria (fig. 10) erected in a very short time under Amri and Achab about 875 (3 Kings 16. 24). The plan is regular, the walls rectilinear, the angles almost perfect right angles. The stones were dressed with a chisel with extreme care, the foundation set in a trench which straightened the rock. This technique was already familiar at Ugarit in the thirteenth century, and there is no doubt that it was introduced into Palestine by foremen and stone-dressers from Tyre. A few specimens of minor importance show that it penetrated into the kingdom of Juda, but was abandoned under the dynasty of Jehu.

In Samaria the "casemated" walls were capable of supporting imposing superstructures, but no attempt was made to erect flankers. On the flat top, shops (*b*) can be made out and a palace which overlooks the paved courtyard (*a*). Although this is larger than the buildings of the same kind already mentioned, it in no way differs from them in principle. The gate of this citadel must have been in the eastern wall, but it has been completely destroyed. The town, in which the common people lived, extended all round on an equivalent surface and was itself surrounded by a wall, but it is not possible to give a plan of this.

Earlier in date than the Samaria buildings, the Salomonic stables of Megiddo were less imposing but yet worthy of interest (fig. 8, *d, e,* and fig. 11). They were rectangular rooms with a central avenue with cement floor and two paved lateral sections where the horses were. In front of each horse was a stone manger held in place between two square pillars which served to support the roof. A hole in the angle of the pillar was used to pass the head-stall through, as is still done in this part of the world. These stables were grouped around large yards and in all they provided lodgings for 450 horses; they remained in use until the end of the dynasty of Amri.

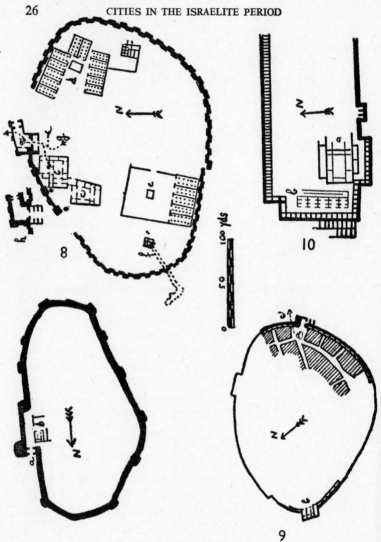

FIG. 7. MIZPA
FIG. 8. MEGIDDO
FIG. 9. TELL BEIT MIRSIM
FIG. 10. SAMARIA

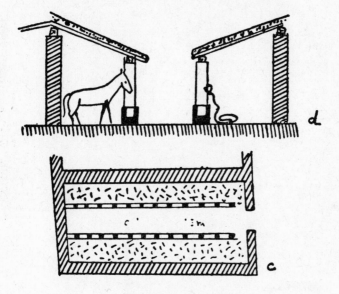

FIG. 11. STABLES OF MEGIDDO

TUNNELS

One of the most spectacular achievements of the Canaanites was the excavation of underground galleries for the purpose of connecting the town within the walls with a spring necessarily situated at a lower level. Several such are known today, in particular that of Megiddo which has formed the subject of an intensive scientific excavation (fig. 8, *f*). It consisted of a large square well surrounded by a spiral stairway and of a practically horizontal gallery leading to the cave in which the spring was flowing. This work can be dated from Iron Age I, the period at which the Canaanites of Megiddo felt the need of strengthening their defences and protecting themselves from blockade. The same date is indicated for other places and may legitimately be taken as general. After a period of neglect the Megiddo gallery was restored under Solomon.

While it is not necessarily the best preserved or even the one most studied, the *sinnor* of Jerusalem (to give it its biblical name which has come into current use among scholars) will perhaps present more interest for the reader. It gave access from inside the city to the spring of Gihon situated near the Cedron (fig. 17, *n*, and fig. 12).

The spring wells up in a cave which has been slightly reconstructed (fig. 12, *a*). Its natural outlet was barred by a thick wall (*b*) and the waters thrust back into the interior of the hill. A gallery enlarging the natural channels conveyed them to a cave (*c*) prolonged by a vertical chimney (*c-d*). From this point a long horizontal gallery (*d-f*) opened, the angular pattern of which is doubtless explained by the quality of the stone beds; then a fairly steep stone stairway was followed as far as the chamber (*g*) covered with a vault late in date. It has not proved possible to follow the underground tunnel as far as the interior of the ancient wall, the pattern of which in this quarter of the city is fairly well known, but it should not be forgotten that the permanent peopling of Jerusalem has destroyed a good deal, and, moreover, the process of excavations in mine galleries used in these investigations brings with it the risk of loss of many details. It must then be assumed that in one way or another the Canaanites of Jerusalem had access to the gallery (*f-d*) without danger and drew their water directly from the flooded cave (*c*). According to tradition, or perhaps the folklore of Israelite Jerusalem, it was through this passage that one of David's companions took the city (2 Kings, 5. 8; cf. 1 Paral. 11. 6).

In the security of the time of the Kings these installations were abandoned. A channel was dug in the hillside (*h*), sometimes underground, sometimes in the open, whence the gardeners of the Cedron might draw water. It led into a large reservoir (*l*) formed by blocking a secondary valley. When the major wars returned, much more important works, of which no equivalent has been found, were undertaken: King Ezechias had a long subterranean channel (*j*) opened to the

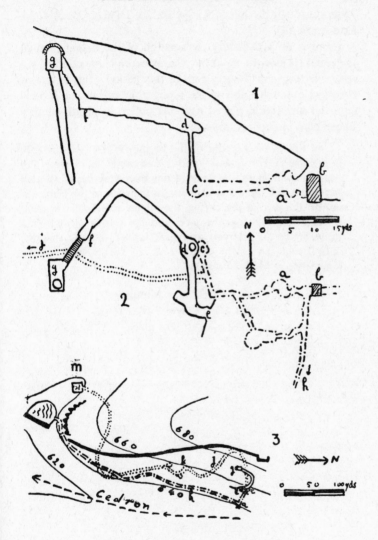

FIG. 12. THE JERUSALEM SINNOR
After H. Vincent, *Underground Jerusalem*

waters through the hill (4 Kings, 20. 20, 2 Paral. 32. 3, 4, 30, Ecclus. 48. 19).

There is no satisfactory explanation of the zigzag plan of the canal (j), nor do we know what was the connection of the reservoir (m) with the city wall of this period—this is one of the most obscure points of the topography of ancient Jerusalem. An inscription placed near the outlet, in eighth-century Phoenician characters, says:

> And this is the account of the boring. Whilst . . . the pick of one (sounded) against another and when there were still three cubits to bore, the voice of one man shouting to another was heard, for there was a fissure in the rock to the right . . . and on the day of the boring, the miners struck one in front of the other, pick against pick, and the waters passed from the spring to the reservoir over 1,200 cubits (650 yds. in exact figures) and the height of the rock above the head of the miners was a hundred cubits.

Even today we can pass through the tunnel, see the hesitations of the two gangs when they are near to meeting (k) and observe the trace of the pick strokes made in both directions.

CHAPTER III

CITIES IN THE HELLENISTIC PERIOD

The conquest of the East by the Macedonians was followed by an economic movement of considerable impetus and by the introduction of numerous new technical devices. Ancient procedure and custom were not, however, totally eliminated, and the result is a great variety for this period. Most fortunately for us, the régime of the semi-autonomous city dear to Greek tradition allowed each community to retain its own character, and it is possible for us to give some clearly differentiated examples.

NATIVE

The population of the small town of Marisa on the confines of the mountains of Juda and the coastal plain was Idumaean, interspersed with a few Phoenician commercial families, and was thus Semitic, although slightly tinged with Hellenism. The names discovered in a necropolis fairly rich in inscriptions provide us with information on this point. Its architecture clearly preserves native features (figs. 14 and 16). The city wall, built without any regard to appearance, is flanked by square towers projecting considerably, a development already begun in the time of the Kings of Israel and Juda. The streets form a very irregular chequer pattern with large divisions, each of which contains an inextricable dovetailing of small houses and yards, in accordance with the most ancient native tradition.

The walls, however, are parallel, the corners squared and the workmanship more correct than in earlier periods; thus there had been progress in technique alone. To the west may be seen a square (a) surrounded by planned buildings probably destined for public use. The small central building must have been a Syrian temple with three niche-recesses, corresponding to the ideas in fashion in the Hellenistic Orient. One gate led directly from the square into the open country. Another gate would seem to have been placed in the south wall of the town, but it is too ruined to allow us to assert this. The whole group (a) apparently corresponds to the introduction by the Greeks of regulated municipal life.

In the block of houses (b) the plans of individual houses can be made out with a sufficient degree of certainty (fig. 16). Still for the same reason, lack of timber, they continued to build houses with a courtyard surrounded by rooms. In (a) can be seen a small house with a central courtyard. The new feature, common at this particular period, is that it is entered through a covered vestibule. In (b) there are two small two-roomed houses, the inner room getting daylight through the adjacent one (cf. Luke 15. 8: a woman lights her lamp to look for a coin); in (c) is a larger house, built perhaps at several different times. In (d) we see a large house with a central courtyard surrounded by an outer courtyard. As regards its dimensions it was equivalent to a "palace" of the Iron Age, and we may think of the dwelling of a rich merchant with facilities for receiving caravans in his house, as was still done in Jerusalem less than a century ago (f); a larger courtyard surrounded by small rooms and by a mediocre dwelling might be a hostelry. These plans give us the picture of a complex society in which new activities and new *élites* have been superimposed upon the traditional background.

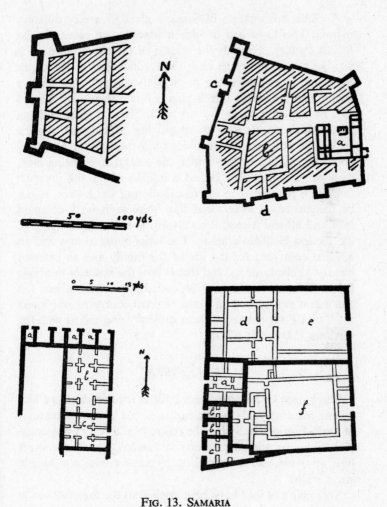

FIG. 13. SAMARIA
FIG. 14. MARISA
FIG. 15. After Crowfoot, *Samaria-Sebaste,* vol. I
FIG. 16. After Bliss and Macalister, *Excavations in Palestine*

SAMARIA

A Hellenistic stratum of Samaria gives us a very different picture. This town had become a Macedonian colony in the fourth century. Towards the middle of the second century it was judged necessary to raise the fortifications of the upper town and to re-establish a residential quarter there. Thus a simple and systematic Greek plan is found there (figs. 13 and 15). In this case again the city wall, between eight and ten yards thick, is flanked by projecting rectangular towers. Inside the walls the city is divided into rectangular blocks of about twenty-five by fifty yards, the central street being lined with shops (15, *a*). The ruined condition of the site prevents our being positive as to the distribution of the houses. It can be recognized, however, that they were built on a common area and all had a central courtyard. It is the typical plan of the modest Hellenistic house. The large house always had an internal courtyard for the life of the family and an external one for public business, and that is how the house of the High Priest Caiaphas must be represented; the room where the Sanhedrin met opened on to the external courtyard and it was there that Peter entered without difficulty and mixed with the servants (Matt. 26. 57–75).

HELLENISTIC

The largest Greek cities were built in regular blocks of fifty by one hundred yards, as is clearly attested by the excavations of Dura-Europos in Syria. The centre of the blocks was occupied by houses with large courtyards connected with the street by a vestibule, and the periphery by smaller houses or simple street stalls.

This plan can well have been applied to the majority of the Arab towns of the Middle Ages. It has been recognized that the present irregularity of their planning came from the progressive degeneration of the ancient geometrical pattern. This was the case at Damascus in particular, whose situation on a plain lent itself to the greatest simplicity (fig. 18): (a) Temple of Zeus, the ancient Aramean Hadad; beneath the Greek architectural and decorative technique there persists the traditional Semitic lay-out in which successive enclosures determine zones of increasing sanctity. After being used for a Christian church, this site is today occupied by the famous mosque of the Ommeyades; (b) the agora, a square surrounded by a wall with porticoes, which was used for the market, for the meeting of the popular assembly and for all the activities of social life; (c) was, according to information from Arab sources, the ancient quarter of the Nabateans, subjects of King Aretas (2 Cor. 11. 32), but the souvenirs of St Paul shown there seem purely conventional; (d) the Straight Street (Acts 9. 11) is still the principal artery of old Damascus.

JERUSALEM

The situation of ancient Jerusalem, built on three well-defined hills, did not lend itself to such simplicity. Its historical development implies that there were quarters of different style. That, however, is a subject of controversy into which we cannot enter here. It is possible, however, to form a general impression of Jerusalem in New Testament times by relying on the science of topography, on such eye-witness observations as are still possible, on the abundant literary data left by the Jewish historian Flavius Josephus, and on the most authentic Christian traditions (fig. 17): (a) the Temple, enlarged and beautified by Herod, occupied the site of the present Haram esh-Sherif. It was flanked on the north by the fortress of Antonia, which overlooked the several courtyards and protected the town (b, schema). There was situated the Roman garrison post which rescued Paul from the anger of the Jews (Acts 21. 27–37). It is likewise possible that Pilate installed himself there in Herod's former apartments. In the northern suburb was situated the pool of Bethsaida (c) (John 5. 2). It consisted of two basins surrounded by a quadrangular portico and separated by a fifth portico. The remains of these buildings have been discovered, as have also the foundations of the Christian churches erected upon them. The sites of Calvary and of the Holy Sepulchre as they have been accepted by Christians since the earliest times of their freedom were at (d) outside the walls. In the present building some remains of the constructions of the Emperor Constantine can be found. The city was protected on the north by two successive walls (somewhat schematized). In the north-west angle of the first wall was Herod's fortified palace (e). The first storey of one of his towers which local tradition calls the "Tower of David" can still be seen. After the fall of the dynasty this palace, more recent in date and more handsome than the Antonia, became the normal residence of the Roman procurator when in Jerusalem. The old palace of the Hasmonean kings, the descendants of Simon Machabeus, was towards point (f). It was later the residence of the Herodian princes (Luke 23. 7–12). The central valley called in Greek "Tyropeon" (Valley of the Cheesemakers) was crossed by an embanked causeway (g) and by a bridge (h). The Temple was thus placed in communication with the western hill or "Upper City". There was the agora figured somewhat arbitrarily in (j). According to the most ancient Christian tradition the Cenacle and the House of Caiaphas were a little more to the south, towards (k). One of the streets of steps which came down from there to the "Tyropeon" has been discovered. It ended a little above the pool of Siloe (l-John 9). The hill situated more to the east and to the south of the Temple was the most ancient heart of the city. A quarter in native style must be imagined there. Towards point (m) the foundation inscription of a synagogue has been discovered, in which it is possible to recognize the "synagogue of the Freedmen" of Acts 6. 9. The founder in fact bears a Latin name, probably that of his former master, according to a common custom. Outside the city the ancient spring of Gihon was at (n). The canal of Ezechias brought its

waters into the pool of Siloe. In the liturgy of the feast of
Tabernacles a procession made its way there to draw the
water which was then taken back to the Temple. The other
natural water point was further down (*p*), this was the ancient
well of the Fuller or Enrogel (3 Kings 1. 9). Reliable Christian
tradition fixes the whereabouts of Haceldama beyond the
valley of Gehenna, towards point (*q*). Several ancient tombs
may be observed there (Matt. 27. 8). Gethsemani was beyond
the Cedron where the foundations of a Byzantine church have
been discovered.

It has been possible to confirm the fact that the Jerusalem
of the New Testament was a beautiful city. In addition to the
Temple, it had palaces, rich houses, works of art, quarters
constructed on a regular plan. We must not, however, imagine
a luxurious construction; the generality of the discoveries of
this period would preclude such a supposition. Only the

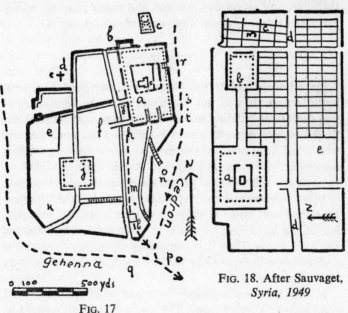

FIG. 17

FIG. 18. After Sauvaget,
Syria, 1949

richest houses were covered with tiles, for all the others the ancient covering of reeds and beaten earth, easy to take to pieces and put together again (Mark 2. 4) was considered sufficient. Only the Temples, the royal buildings and the fortifications were built of dressed stone; in ordinary circumstances people were satisfied with large quarry stones unchiselled or quarried in the mass, the spaces in between being filled by smaller stones, and the whole bound together by mortar made of clay. At most, the doors were bordered by a series of dressed stones. To improve the appearance of these walls and protect them against severe weather, they were coated with clay mixed with a little chalk. On the inside such coatings were finer and could be covered with paintings. Even when a rich man embellished his house with a few stone pillars, they were cut of limestone of indifferent quality and covered with stucco. The thresholds were constructed of one large piece of stone well worked, the floors were of beaten earth or of paving stone, mosaics were extremely rare.

JERICHO

On all these points the Roman era witnessed a general improvement. It was not, however, until the Middle Ages that the art of building underwent an important transformation: the application to private buildings of the stone vaulting which had been used for centuries in public buildings. When compared with ancient times the Arabic East provided an example of both technical progress and decadence in the sense of urban agglomerations: the *souk* or shopping street, derived from the Greek street of shops; it was often covered, however, and at the same time narrowed by progressive inroads of the public highway. Thus it is completely erroneous to represent ancient towns in accordance with the aspect of the old quarters of the towns of today.

In the Hellenistic period the royal buildings underwent considerable development. The demand for elegance and comfort was combined with a need for defensive strength; and the two best known examples illustrate these two particular preoccupations.

In the environs of Jericho Herod the Great had a pleasure palace where he died. It was considerably enlarged by his son Archelaus, then pillaged in the course of the disturbances which brought his reign to an end. Abandoned from that time onwards, it was used as a quarry for the neighbouring city. Thus only the foundations have been discovered but they are sufficiently revealing to allow of a partial reconstruction of the principal buildings (fig. 19).

The first palace (a) was built according to the principle of the Hellenistic house with two courtyards. Some architectural debris, drums of columns, Ionian and Corinthian capitals show a fairly highly developed attempt at decoration despite the roughness of masonry that is extremely poor in quality. A little later, a small, ancient fort (c) served as the foundation for a superimposed pavilion. The upper parts of the masonry have disappeared, but abundant debris of decorative revetments in baked clay or in moulded plaster permit of no doubt as to their existence. Later still Archelaus had a more imposing ensemble erected: on the side of a small valley where a little water flowed from time to time, a long terrace wall (b-b) supported an esplanade on which no doubt gardens were planted. This wall was ornamented with niches where statues might be placed and in the centre it opened into a small theatre. The base was bordered by a long narrow trough of water, a device of which no other example is known and which leaves room for some hesitation as to detail. At the two extremities of the wall (b) sub-foundations for the strongly vaulted basement rooms have been found, apparently made to support one or several floors which have entirely disappeared. One of these cellars received a jet of water and could be arranged as an artificial grotto. The whole of this construction was carried out in accordance with the Roman technique of the *opus reticulatum*: concrete grouted by hand between two walls of small stones. There is thus no doubt that the builders were brought back from Italy on the occasion of some journey. The water came from a spring in the neighbouring mountain through an aqueduct which, after certain repairs, is still in use. One arm supplied water to the buildings and gardens described, the other rendered the same services on the opposite bank, where it has only been possible to discover unidentifiable remains. From the top of the pavilion or from the steps of the theatre could be seen the view of the gardens which extended into the beautiful Jericho oasis. In the distance the tawny mountains and the striking marly ground of the plain made this patch of green stand out more vividly. This close union of architecture and landscape show

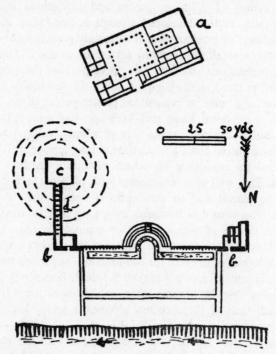

FIG. 19. After Kelso and Baramki, *Excavations at New Testament Jericho*

Italian influence, as does the construction; it is known that the Romans excelled at it.

In Gospel times, the traveller who went up from Jericho to Jerusalem passed quite close to these ruins and could meditate on the vanity of attempts at an earthly paradise. He could also remind himself that their founder himself had made a hell of them. To recall only one of the sinister stories connected with these places, it was in the great reservoir which served as a bathing-pool for his palace that Herod contrived the drowning of his young brother-in-law, Aristobulus, a descendant of the Hasmonean kings. He feared his popularity.

MASADA

FIG. 20. MASADA: From above

Some of the royal fortresses were situated in the city, but many others were in the open country, which is characteristic of the period. Certain of these castles were of strategic importance: by overlooking some vital passage they effectively protected a whole province. Others, however, were destined solely for the personal security of the prince. Situated in the open desert, along little used routes, they were at the same time a safe place for his treasures, a refuge for him and his family, and a halting place on the way to foreign countries. The best preserved and most impressive of these fortresses is that of Masada, situated on a fragment of the plateau of Idumaea, detached from the mass by a cleft of more than 100 yards, and on the other side overlooking by 400 yards the marly ledge which goes alongside the Dead Sea. It commanded two routes towards Arabia, to the south and south-east (fig. 20, after an aerial view taken from the east).

The only access to Masada was by a zigzag path (*k*) which made assault and the use of war machines impossible. It was so richly stocked that the Jewish zealots who occupied it were enabled to sustain the blockade of the Romans for a year (fig. 20, *l*, rampart wall and redoubts). The latter finally brought matters to a head by piling up an enormous earthwork (*m*).

The plateau, with a surface of about twenty acres, was surrounded by a casemated wall strengthened at intervals by towers. Distributed irregularly over the surface were shops, long narrow chambers, and single or communal dwelling places constructed on the common principle of the courtyard surrounded by rooms (fig. 21, *d-j*). Numerous cisterns scattered over the plateau received the rain water. Two aqueducts (*n* and *p*) which took the water from the dams of the valleys and conveyed it into large underground reservoirs half way up the slope (not shown) were added. This latter work was, according to all probability, the personal work of Herod who had inherited the fortress from his father. To him also can be attributed the embellishment of a small dwelling paved in mosaic paving stones, very rare at that period. By about sixty-five feet it dominated a curious circular building perched on a ledge of rock, the use of which it has not been possible to determine. Lower still, a third ledge supported a square pavilion ornamented by a double peristyle with arcades and columns. It was decorated with stucco painted with veining and in panels of bright colours. There could be enjoyed the coolness of the evening breeze and an extensive view over the Dead Sea. Stairways, half constructed and half hollowed out

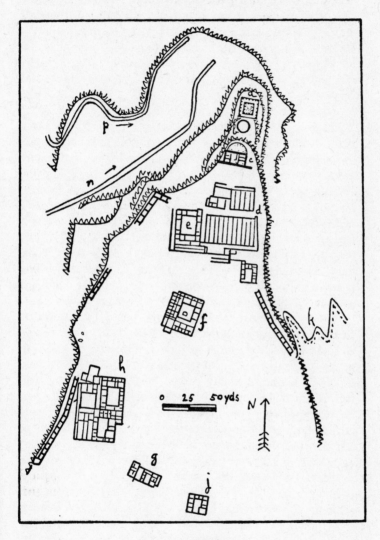

FIG. 21. MASADA
After "Masada". Israel Exploration Society

of the rock, connected the three terraces. This concern for architectural skill and refinement in a brigands' den reflects the spirit of the Herodian royalty.

CHAPTER IV

RELIGIOUS ARCHITECTURE

PRIMITIVE: OPEN AIR SANCTUARIES

The most ancient sanctuaries contemporary with the patriarchs were erected in the open air. They usually comprised a commemorative stele, an altar for the sacrifices and frequently a large tree—an evergreen oak or a turpentine tree—the permanent foliage of which gave beauty to the site and provided a symbol of the continual goodwill of God (Gen. 28. 18; 35. 7–15, Josue 24. 25–28). This form of sanctuary was borrowed from the old Canaanite civilization, and one of the finest examples has been found in the ancient town of Gezer (Josue 10. 33). It dates back to a very remote antiquity and remained in use until far into the Iron Age, most probably until the acquisition of the town by Solomon (3 Kings 9. 16).

The most sacred place was a natural grotto approached by a stairway cut into the rock (fig. 22, *a*). In the centre were the remains of the sacrifice of a child (*b*), an artificial hole (*c*) provided communication between this cave, dwelling-place of the gods beneath the earth, and the surface. It could be used for libations. To the west of the grotto was the altar (*d*) made of a large single piece of stone dressed and hollowed into the shape of a trough. In front of it on a paved platform was erected a line of steles, large stones roughly quarried and three or six feet in height. Two round constructions (*f*) served as depositories for the offerings of the faithful, whether pottery or figurines, several cisterns provided water (*g*), and there was also a storeplace for the bones of animal or human victims. Over the surface generally were burial places of children and small offerings, pottery, bronze jewellery and various figurines, some of which were clearly connected with the fertility cults which in ancient Mediterranean times were always associated with the gods of the underworld.

Even among the Israelites and after the foundation of the Temple of Jerusalem more or less impure cults continued to be practised in the open air. It has already been said that the royal city of Tirza had near its gate a stele and a pool for ablutions (pp. 22, 23). On the hills to the west of Jerusalem have been found several of the high places which were severely stigmatized by the prophets. One of them has been entirely uncovered (fig. 23).

It is a large circular enclosure bordered by a wall of undressed stones fairly carefully joined together. Access to the interior was by two staircases, one on the east, the other on the north-west (*a, b*). Opposite the stairway on the east it has been possible to identify a paved platform surrounded by low walls of loose stones, with a small trench (*c*) surrounded by flat stones which could be used to receive the blood of the victims. The site of the hearth must have been at (*d*) where a quantity of ashes was found. Numerous pottery fragments enable us to date this sanctuary from the time of the last kings of Juda, contemporary with the prophets. The whole installation was covered with a heap of stones a little over eighteen feet high, in which it is possible to recognize the work of the pious king Josias, destroyer of the high places (4 Kings 23. 5-20). The specialists, moreover, are uncertain about the exact character of the worship performed in these places, since such moderately simple installations can be adapted to quite different religious rites. No stele, image or divine figurine of any sort has been found, and even today the Samaritans of Nablus celebrate the Pasch in a small rustic sanctuary very similar to that which has just been described: a rectangular enclosure of rough stones, trenches and hearths very simply installed; and such worship, of course, is in no way contrary to the strictest monotheism.

MIDDLE BRONZE: THE HOUSE FOR THE GOD

Fairly early, also, people conceived the idea of building houses for the gods, and excavations have made certain of these known to us. One of them has recently been discovered, with its outbuildings, near Nahariya in Israel. Here it can be seen that the building of a house did not do away with all the elements of the open-air sanctuaries (fig. 24). In its best attested state the temple properly so-called was a rectangular building of thirty-three by eighteen feet. Its framework was sustained by wooden pillars, the sockets of which have been found. A single door provided an opening on the long side— the most usual arrangement in the Bronze Ages (*a*). Outside was a heap of stones about three feet high, to which access was provided by a stairway (*b*). There small votive objects were deposited, and traces of organic matter also suggest oil libations. Some analogy can thus be found between this pile and the altars of undressed stones prescribed by the law of Moses (Exod. 20. 25). Not far away a shallow trench (*c*) served to collect the blood of the victims. The hearth has not been discovered.

One example is known of a subterranean temple being used in the same way as a natural grotto; this is at Tirza. It is a rectangular chamber, fifteen feet by twelve, fitted with a bench where offerings of pottery were deposited, by the side of which were found the bones of sacrificed animals. This pottery is typical Middle Bronze Age, whereas the geometrical level of the chamber is that of previous eras. This justifies us in concluding that an underground cavity was artificially hollowed out.

The objects which are found in the interior of the temples are usually votive objects similar to those of the open-air sanctuaries. On one occasion at least votive steles have been found, at Hazor, a large and famous Canaanite city (Josue 11), in a small rectangular temple very badly built (fig. 25). The back wall is hollowed out into an apse preceded by a platform where there were several basalt steles of fine work-manship, one of them representing two hands extending towards the crescent moon. At the side was the statuette of a man seated, without any divine insignia. It was probably a worshipper taking part in the feast which followed the sacri-fices. In front was a stone table for offerings and several pieces of pottery (fig. 26).

This last example shows clearly that the steles were not looked upon as the sign of a divine presence, but as the memorial of a human presence; the two uplifted hands repre-sent the man in prayer and the wording of the inscriptions which are found in fairly large numbers in the late periods points to the same conclusion. Memorials might also be made of some special intervention of the divinity: among the steles of a temple at Gebal (Byblos) was found a ship's anchor dedicated by some sailor. As has been suggested, the steles of the old Israelite sanctuaries exercised a similar function. There was nothing in this contrary in principle to monotheism, but in actual fact this ancient custom was linked to polytheism, and for this reason it was reproved by the prophets.

IRON AGE I: THE ISRAELITE TEMPLES

When the Israelites constructed temples in the period of the Judges (Judges 17. 5, 18. 27–30, 1 Kings 1. 7, 21. 1–7) these buildings cannot have been much different from what the Canaanites had produced. Solomon, however, had his con-structed on other principles. Despite certain difficulties in the text, the description given us in the Book of Kings is easy to understand in its general principles (3 Kings 5. 15; 6. 38): a porch wider than it was deep was followed by a hall, the "Holy Place" or "Hekal", and by a second one, the "Holy of Holies" or "Debir", which contained the Ark of the Cov-enant. This architectural plan was well known in Anatolia in the Late Bronze Age. From there it spread to Canaan, and the excavations at Hazor have provided an example of it. The best archaeological parallel to the work of Solomon,

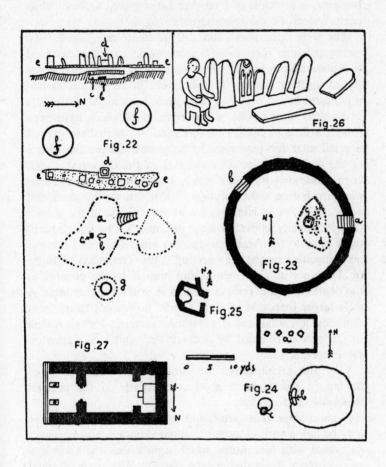

SANCTUARIES
FIG. 22. After Macalister, *The Excavation of Gezer*
FIG. 23. After R. Amiran, *Israel Exploration Journal, No. 8*
FIG. 24. After Dothan, *Israel Exploration Journal, No. 6*
FIGS. 25 and 26. After Yadin—Hazor
FIG. 27. After McEwan, *American Journal of Archaeology, 1937*

however, is a temple of Iron Age I discovered at Tell Tainat near Antioch on the lower Orontes (fig. 27).

The wide open porch can still be easily recognized. Two strong columns supported its framework; they corresponded to Solomon's columns "Yakin" and "Boaz" (these two words joined together mean: "It holds well!"). In the further hall a platform breast high had supported the colossal statue of a god seated on a throne, a few remains of which have been found; a little in front a smaller platform must have carried a small altar for perfumes. In Solomon's temple the throne of the god was replaced by the Ark of the Covenant, and it is probable that the latter was not deposited on an artificial platform but on the projecting rock which the Moslems still venerate in the building known as the "Dome of the Rock" (and incorrectly as the "Mosque of Omar"). The Jewish traditions prior to the Arab construction are definite and there is no compelling reason for rejecting them. The vision of Isaias (6. 1) shows us God manifesting himself to the prophet in the confines of the Temple such as it existed at that time. A little larger than that of Tell Tainat, Solomon's temple was doubtless less solid, and it was almost certainly for this reason that it was surrounded by a casemated wall with rooms on three storeys.

Like the architecture, the furniture and decoration of Solomon's temple have good counterparts in the oriental milieu of the Iron Age.

Stone incense altars are found in large numbers. The table may be half a yard at most measured sideways, and is always decorated with four horns which signify that the altar is a sacred object, if not divine even (fig. 28). The altars of metal were made on the same pattern (Exod. 37. 25-9).

An example of a bronze chariot, intended for the carrying of large receptacles, is known; it was discovered in Cyprus (fig. 29). It is a framework strengthened by panels and by oblique cross-pieces and carried on four wheels; the top is open with a round hole and strengthened by a circular crown;

panels and crown are decorated with interlacing and with
imaginary animals.

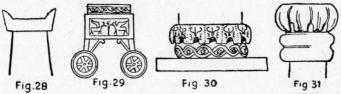

Fig.28   Fig.29   Fig 30   Fig 31

The temple of Tell Tainat shows bases of columns decorated
with garlands and interlacing as well as a capital in the form
of a flower with drooping petals which are an indication of
the decorative style of the two columns of Jerusalem (figs.
30, 31).

The purely decorative features are also well represented.
The cherubim of the Ark (Exod. 25. 18) are derived from an
ancient Egyptian theme often adopted in Phoenician art contemporary with the kings of Israel (fig. 33). According to
common Egyptian custom, the wings are attached to the arms,
the movement of which they follow, but a special feature in
Phoenician and Syrian art is the development of the feathers
into a kind of corselet. This imitation, though elegant, leads
to some inconsistency; the cherubim on the right has an open
hand to which a lotus flower is attached, it is not quite clear
how.

The Cherubim which ornamented the Holy of Holies were
much larger, placed frontwise and side by side (3 Kings 6.
23-8); according to Isaias they had six wings, which gives
them a certain resemblance to a representation found in Upper
Syria which can be dated from about the tenth century (fig.
32). If it were possible to interpret the kind of ribbons coming
from the head as flames, the figure could more accurately be
termed a Seraphim, that is, a "Being of Fire", as in Isaias.
Later in this book other examples will be found of this art
of Tell Halaf in which the tradition of Upper Mesopotamia
is placed at the service of a very young Aramean kingdom.
Despite its rough workmanship, it is really animated.

FIGS. 32–36. PHOENICIAN IVORIES
After Decamps de Merzenfeld

Cherubim were used also to decorate the accessories of the Temple along with lions, bulls, palm-leaves and scrolls (3 Kings 7. 29, 36). These Cherubim were similar to those fantastic winged beings found in Mesopotamian art, arbitrarily endowed with all the most terrible functions of nature—the horns of the bull, the teeth and claws of the lion, beak and talons of the eagle, the scorpion's tail, and even the head of a man. Already of long standing in Syria, this art had been enriched by Egyptian themes and had adopted the characteristics of the local style—elegant, static, somewhat academic. Since we know that the work of the temple of Jerusalem was carried out by Tyrian artists (3 Kings 7, 13, 40-7), its decoration must be imagined in accordance with the examples provided by certain Syrian or Phoenician ivories (fig. 34, body and claws of lion, ram's head wearing the Egyptian crown and the solar disc, scorpion's tail; fig. 35: sphinx with woman's head; fig. 36: gryphon with bird's head and body of a lion).

The only information available on Herod's temple is from literary documents. There is no difficulty in deducing from them the general outline of the temple and of the courts; most editions of the Bible give such a plan. The adaptation of the site, however, remains problematical. What we have suggested in fig. 17 corresponds to hypotheses that cannot be discussed here. Only the outer enclosure, due entirely to Herod, is still to be seen and thus provides us with certainty. A few remarks will be made later in this book as to its decoration, in the discussion on funerary art.

Nothing is left of the first synagogues of Palestine, those in which our Lord was accustomed to speak to the people (Matt. 4. 23, etc.). One of those of the Hellenic diaspora has, however,

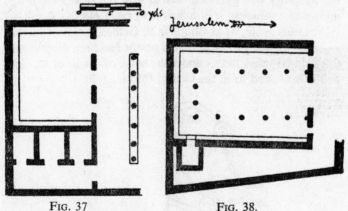

FIG. 37   FIG. 38.
After Sukenik, *Ancient Synagogues*

been discovered at Delos, which was a centre of international commerce where an important Jewish community resided (1 Mach. 15. 23: fig. 37). The most ancient synagogues discovered in Galilee date from the end of the third century. They were still constructed according to the same principles (fig. 38), though rather more monumental in style. Thus the synagogues of the Gospel were similar, but more modest in their architecture.

In the two examples given, the synagogue is a rectangular hall with benches on three sides. The doors were inserted on the remaining side, that of Jerusalem. The people prayed turning towards the Holy City and if it was impossible to see it, it was at least possible to imagine that no obstacle was interposed between the faithful and the dwelling which God himself had chosen (this custom is already attested in Daniel 6.11). There was no emplacement reserved for the holy books. It was doubtless in the course of the fourth century that the custom of making a decorated cupboard for them, often placed in a small apse, and of praying in this direction, was introduced into Palestine. As a consequence the orientation of the buildings was modified, but to save the reader from any danger of confusion, it is sufficient to point out this detail.

At Delos again, as at Chorazin in Galilee, a seat of honour reserved for the president or the orator has been discovered: the Talmud refers to this under the name of "chair of Moses", and it is alluded to in the Gospel (Matt. 23. 2).

FIG. 39.

FIG. 40.

That at Delos is an armchair of marble very similar to those set aside for important personages in the theatre; it is a fine example of Hellenistic furniture. That of Chorazin (fig. 40) is a block of local basalt of rather rough workmanship, the arms and the small back rest appear to be imitated from the folding seats in use at the time.

It was perhaps in the synagogues or in connection with them that Jewish religious art was born and developed. It may be

FIG. 41   FIG. 42

recognized from the use of subjects drawn from the liturgy of the Temple to decorate various objects, lamps, dishes, etc., etc.

Such are in fig. 41 the Temple itself, a palm from the liturgy of the feast of Tabernacles (Lev. 23. 40) and a small shovel for burning incense. In fig. 42: the seven-branched candlestick, an incense shovel, and the horn trumpet inherited from the ancient liturgy of the Ark (Josue 6. 5). The lamp of fig. 42 is of the second century and, as a general rule, the art we are speaking of developed from the third century. Lamp 41, however, is of "Herodian" shape and is still connected with the period that interests us. It would seem that after the destruction of the Temple certain of these objects passed into the synagogue ritual, and that people were anxious to represent them all.

A few remarks must be made about the Monastery of the Essenes of Qumrân. In actual fact, the importance of the discoveries on the shores of the Dead Sea is essentially literary, which puts them outside the limits of this book. Briefly, it can be said that the discovery of an almost complete roll of Isaias as well as innumerable biblical fragments is a very important contribution to the establishment of the text. The new readings, moreover, remain within the already known gap between the Hebrew, the Greek and the Samaritan texts, but they sometimes confirm one of the two latter against the Massoretic. Moreover, the discovery of numerous para-biblical texts, whole or in fragments, adds to our knowledge of the Jewish background, all the more so in that several of them were totally unknown while others have only come down to us in translation.

It is at this point that material archaeology intervenes. Writings only develop their full interest if it is possible to date them. Ours contain no indication of this kind and their allusions to general history are most obscure. Thus the first publications left scholars in considerable uncertainty. It was only two years later, in 1949, that the first cave was scientifically excavated and that the presence of a considerable quantity of Hellenistic pottery pointed to centuries earlier than the Christian era. Other caves containing similar pottery and fragments of writing were then discovered. They extended in all directions around a ruin called "Khirbet Qumrân" which it was then considered necessary to excavate. The same kind of pottery was found there and, in addition, numerous coins which made it possible to assign an exact date to it: a first period of habitation lasted from the reign of Alexander Janneus to that of Herod, i.e. from 100–31 B.C. An earthquake put an end to this; a second period lasted from the reign of Archelaus to the destruction of the site by the Romans, that is, from A.D. 1 to 68. Then a small Roman garrison was installed in the ruins for a few years. To the two principal periods correspond the two styles of pottery instanced in the first chapter (pp. 17, 20).

But besides giving us information about the date of the

manuscripts, the excavations have thrown light on the kind
of life and means of existence of the writers of the documents.
They have even made it possible to recognize the name of
their community.

Although situated in a desert region on the shores of the
Dead Sea, the establishment was not without resources. An
hour's walk away, a large spring made it possible to plant a
fine palm grove; and the latest series of excavations there has
shown buildings of the same period and character as the
central installation (fig. 43, *k*). The latter is situated rather
high up, on the marly ledge (43, *c*) which dominates the shore
by about forty yards, and is thus healthier and fresher. The
ledge itself (*c*) extends to the foot of the mountain where there
are several of the caves. All these details agree exactly with
the description Pliny has left us of the Essenian Jews who, he
tells us, led an ascetic and community life on the shores of
the Dead Sea.

The community character of the principal building is clear
from the plan of it (fig. 45, simplified). Despite the presence
of a small tower (*a*) which could be used to keep off marau-
ders, the thin walls and their numerous openings show no
anxiety about defence. The most remarkable feature is the
system for bringing water in and storing it. An aqueduct
conveyed it from a natural pool into which from time to time
a cascade poured. The ancient weir has been swept away but
a small tunnel through which the channel crossed a spur of
rock can still be seen. Then it crossed the plateau where the
trace of it is easily visible (fig. 43, *h*). The water entered a
paved court (fig. 45, *m*), where it spread and deposited the
greater part of its mud, then a canal (shown in dotted lines)
distributed it among six large cisterns and several small basins
not shown. Around this canal were distributed the workshops:
store-rooms, ovens and mills (*k*), dyeing rooms (*d*), washing-
house (*e*), pottery shop (*l*). The rooms were used for community purposes, judging by their dimensions. Room (*b*)
surrounded by a bench of cemented clay could serve for meet-

ings; (c) was surmounted by an upper storey where the workroom of the scribes was situated: their tables, benches and a basin for ritual ablutions were discovered in a confused condition on the ground floor. They were made of unbaked brick covered with cement, a technique which must have been common in a country poor in wood but which had not previously been encountered; inkstands were found in them. The long room (g) was flanked by a pantry (h) containing a quantity of tableware. It must have been used for religious meals and perhaps also for other ceremonies; a paved platform could have been used by the president or orator. Outside were courtyards and dependencies like the long building (j), probably the stable for the asses.

The majority of the members of the community thus lived outside the central building. Some had chosen the natural caves of the mountain. Others had hollowed out shelters on the marly ledge (fig. 43, g, is the window of one of these). One of these shelters has been discovered in a fairly good state of preservation (fig. 44, no scale). Coming down from the plateau along a narrow inclined path and small flights of steps, two underground rooms were found situated in an angle of the ledge which enable several windows to be inserted.

A long wall (fig. 43, f, fig. 45, n) cut off the cemetery whose community character is indicated by the strict alignment of the tombs and their uniformity. They are of the simplest pattern and contain no object at all, however modest, in contrast with the customs of the epoch. About 1,100 of them have been counted, but it would be hazardous to draw conclusions from this as to the strength of the community; for on the one hand nothing is known as to the rate of mortality; on the other, certain documents indicate that there were Essenes living outside the community who may perhaps have liked to be buried in the cemetery.

One cannot refrain from noting the resemblance between the grouping of the Essenes around their centre and that of the Christian monks of the Orient. They, too, liked to live in

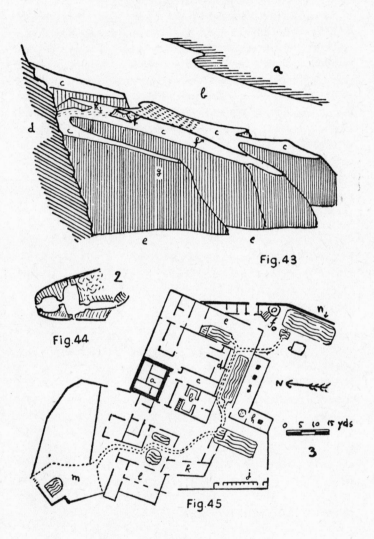

Fig. 43

Fig. 44

Fig. 45

After *Revue Biblique*, 1953, 1956

hermitages or small groups around a convent where they could find the ordinary services and the liturgical assemblies. In the present state of our knowledge it is not impossible to envisage some direct connection; but more probably any convergence is simply due to a community of spirit: a rather pessimistic view of the world and ordinary society, a passionate desire for God sought in meditation rather than in liturgical pomp, the will to heroic asceticism, such tendencies may well have given rise at two different times to analogous structures.

CHAPTER V

FUNERARY ART

MIDDLE AND LATE BRONZE

Canaanite tombs of the Middle and Late Bronze Ages are to be found in fairly large numbers. The most usual type is situated in caves or else they are circular chambers to which access is gained by a vertical shaft. In those most skilfully constructed the shaft was better excavated and provided with a flight of steps and the chambers were of rectangular shape.

A tomb of this kind has been discovered in ancient Jerusalem (fig. 17, not far from *m*). It has been possible to reconstruct the entrance, thanks to the examples preserved at Megiddo, Ras-Shamra and elsewhere (fig. 50). It is probable that this was the tomb of the early kings of Jerusalem, and it is possible that it was used for David after them, since it is said that he was interred in the city (3 Kings 2. 10).

EARLY ISRAELITE

Of the earliest Israelite times, nothing has been found. The exploration of Palestine is today sufficiently developed for it to be possible to draw a conclusion from this negative fact: the large majority of burial-places must have been extremely modest, simple shallow graves which have since been obliterated by tilling or erosion; or else caves and shelters under rocks must have been used for the purpose. A few tombs of this kind have been found on the outskirts of ancient Jerusalem. In the case of the common people this manner of procedure must have continued for a long period, since at the close of the time of the Kings common burial pits were still in use (4 Kings 23. 6; Jerem. 26. 23).

ERA OF THE KINGS

About the close of Iron Age I, thus at the close of the era of the Kings, family tombs began to be found. One of these, near the village of Edh-Dhahiriya, already shows the principles which were to predominate in the future. The tomb is entered through an opening in the hillside by going down a few steps (fig. 49). A little later, in Iron Age II, the customs of equipping funeral chambers with two or three benches arranged in horseshoe fashion prevailed, a fashion that would be maintained in the following eras. In the same period the documents show us the Kings of Juda preparing their burial place outside the town (4 Kings 21. 18). This was still considered a luxury and Isaias (22. 16) reproaches an official of the palace with it. It is possible that this latter tomb has been discovered on the outskirts of Jerusalem. The chamber hollowed out of the rock has been worked over since, but an inscription, the handwriting of which is clearly of the period, is worth quoting:

"This is the tomb of . . . yahu master of the palace. Here there is neither silver nor gold, only his bones and the bones of his servant maid with him. Cursed be the man who opens it."

This formula recalls very closely analogous Phoenician or Aramaic inscriptions. On the question of survival after death, the ideas of the Israelites of that time were no different from those of their neighbours. It was thought of as a kind of reduced existence, comparable to a heavy sleep, from which it was painful to be awakened (1 Kings 28. 15). In a manner which they did not try to define, the mere fact of leaving a dead man unburied was felt to be an insult (4 Kings 9. 25-37, Jerem. 8. 22), and they were convinced that the bones of a prophet could have miraculous power (4 Kings 13. 21).

HELLENISTIC ERA

In the Hellenistic era the model of the previous epoch was at first maintained in every detail, but a more elaborate arrangement was often resorted to.

In a great mausoleum of the first or second century B.C. can be seen an entrance, a central room and three funeral chambers equipped with horseshoe benches to which were added "ovens" each capable of receiving a body (fig. 46, *a, b. c*). The workmanship was still somewhat irregular. In a mausoleum of the Herodian era, smaller, but of more careful workmanship, the benches are equipped with a small ledge and with a head-support (fig. 47). This detail shows that the bodies were buried without a coffin, simply wrapped in linen (John 11. 44 and 20. 5-7). A little later still the benches were inserted under a shallow dome known as the *arcosolium*, the chamber retaining its flat ceiling (fig. 46, *d*). In this case a stone sarcophagus or a coffin of wood or lead was used. The latter arrangement developed in the Roman era and replaced the preceding one.

The great majority of the tombs were closed by a simple slab of masonry, always very small, across the entrance. A few cases of closing by a mill-stone are, however, known. Here we give a somewhat modest example found in Nazareth [fig. 48: the millstone (*a*) moves backwards and forwards in a recess prepared for it and can block or open the door. The funeral chamber is of indifferent workmanship, two "ovens" open out of one wall, another wall has been destroyed].

Moreover, the majority of the tombs were undistinguished by any monument. The Gospel, confirmed by a passage from the Rabbinic traditions, merely tells us that the door was coated with chalk to prevent a passer-by contracting a ritual impurity through inadvertence (Matt. 23. 27). The mausoleums built for the important families, however, had monumental façades carved in the rock. Several of them have been discovered in the immediate neighbourhood of Jerusalem, in

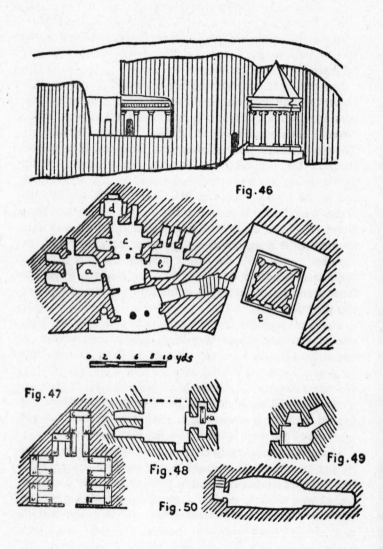

Fig.46

Fig.47

Fig.48

Fig.49

Fig.50

TOMBS

particular in the valley of the Cedron, those which tradition calls "the tombs of Absalom, of Josaphat, of Zacharias and of St James" (fig. 17, *s, t*). In actual fact they were the tombs of priestly families of the first rank. The inscription carried by one of them expressly assigns it to the family of the Bene-Hezir (1 Paral. 24. 15: fig. 46). The mausoleum, already described as to its subterranean part, was ornamented with a façade of Doric type, by the side of which was erected a commemorative monument carved in the rock—a stone cube with Ionic decoration surmounted by an Egyptian cornice and a pyramid. Such combinations are in no way exceptional in Hellenistic funerary architecture.

The dead were interred with certain objects: jewellery, coins, lamps, small jars of perfume or simple pieces of pottery. Those discovered are usually very modest, but the majority of tombs have been pillaged since ancient times. It does happen that jewels of value are found and it must also be remembered that the perfumes were costly. This was a gesture of affection which implied no precise idea of survival. The Jews themselves had divided views on this question (Matt. 22. 23 and elsewhere). Still less was it thought that in his future life the dead man would have the precise use of the objects that were left for him.

HERODIAN PERIOD

The use of stone sarcophagi, which had been known for a very long time in the adjoining countries, only began to be introduced among the Jews in the Herodian period and even so was limited to large and rich mausoleums. They were decorated, as were the lead coffins, with motifs borrowed from the Greco-oriental art of the time (fig. 55). Sufficiently far removed from Greek classicism, this art combined scrolls of foliage with geometrical patterns, in particular, rosettes. It offered a curious mixture of stylization and fantasy and found no difficulty in juxtaposing on a single branch fruits and leaves of different species. In Jewish circles, vegetable designs charged with pagan symbolism were made use of without scruple: the vine and pineapple of Dionysios or the pomegranate of Persephone. Human or animal figures, however, fairly frequent in neighbouring countries, were carefully avoided.

The doors of several monumental mausoleums are decorated in the same style, but in actual fact this art was not specifically funerary in character; it was to be met with in public or private buildings and the descriptions of Herod's temple lead us to imagine a decoration of the same kind.

OSSUARIES

A more popular and perhaps more specifically Jewish art was that of the ossuaries. Since the tombs had to serve for several generations, people had for long been content to pile up the dried bones in a hole when it was necessary to make room. About the time of the New Testament and later the custom was adopted of arranging them in small stone compartments or "ossuaries". They were made of soft limestone easy to engrave with an etching-needle or to hollow out with the chisel (figs. 51–54).

In such decorations architectonic patterns (51) and stylized plants are found (52: branch of olive tree between two rolled palms), and even more frequently rosettes in which the free play of the compass rather than the imitation of some model (54) can be seen, and borders of coils and dots. Certain examples are derived from wooden models (53: panels, feet and rings of a chest). The designs of earlier Jewish iconography (referred to above, p. 55) are never found; perhaps a Jew would have scrupled to associate together a symbol of worship with death, which for him was something radically impure.

As it is very rare for a style of decoration to be limited to one single material or one single category of objects, it is legitimate to suppose that this decoration of Jewish ossuaries is the only remaining vestige of a popular art which usually had to be executed with perishable materials, wood, painting or embroidery.

NAMES

It is exceptional to find inscriptions on the tombs or sarcophagi and when they do exist they seldom yield anything but names. Moreover, it was not the custom of the peoples of Syria to write on stone to any extent, and if they did so it was in letters of an informal nature and of small dimensions.

On the other hand the name of the person whose remains they contained was frequently found on the ossuaries. This custom seems to have increased with time, and perhaps one

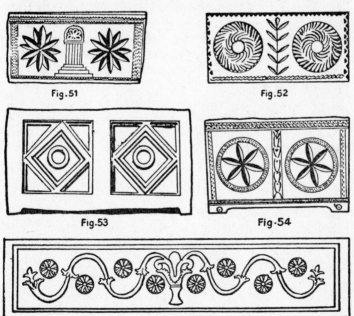

Fig. 51   Fig. 52

Fig. 53   Fig. 54

FIG. 55

should see in it the effect of a more positive idea as to individual survival. The study of these inscriptions, generally cursive and therefore difficult to decipher, is in its beginnings. Already two conclusions seem well established.

One is the diffusion of the Greek language, at least among the inhabitants of Jerusalem: in an important collection recently studied, seven inscriptions are in Hebrew, eleven in Aramaic, eleven in Greek. The group of Hellenists was thus numerous and some are even noted as proselytes, or new converts (Acts 6. 1–7).

Another result is the abundance of names with which the New Testament has made us familiar, again confirming the Jewish and often Palestinian character of this literary ensemble. Once or several times are found: Simon, Simon bar Jona, (Matt. 16. 17), Simon, son of John (John 21. 15), Joseph, Juda, John, Eleazar or Lazarus, Jesus, and even Jesus son of Joseph, Jonathan, Zachary, Jairus, Menahem, Joseph; among the names of women: Salome, Mary, Martha, and once Martha and Mary together, Saphira. It is obvious that the similarities are simply due to the extreme frequency of these names.

CHAPTER VI

COINS

Reference has already been made to the usefulness of coins in dating an archaeological find. They are also of interest in themselves: the choice of coins and inscriptions was not made at random; it reveals something of the tendencies of the prince whose decision it was and of the people for whom such coins and inscriptions were destined.

THE MACHABEES

It is thought that it was Simon Machabaeus who first received the right to coin money (1 Mach. 13. 36-42 and 15. 29). This right never extended to silver coinage, and foreign coins, generally those from Tyre, were constantly in use. Thus Jewish coins are only of bronze and generally of mediocre workmanship; the coin is badly centred on the blank, the letters ill formed and ill set, sometimes faulty.

The first specimens which have come down to us are those of Simon's successor, John Hyrcanus I (134–104). His inscriptions usually run "Jehohanan the High Priest and the community of the Jews", or sometimes: " . . . head of the community . . ." The obverse almost always carries a poppy head between two cornucopias, a symbol of prosperity frequent at the time (fig. 56 *a*). The inscriptions are in Phoenician characters, which were still in current use. It was in the course of the first century that they were replaced by Aramaic or square characters.

Alexander Janneus, son of Hyrcanus, was a prince of

conquest, despotic in character (104–76). His coins carry on one side in Greek: "Alexander King" and on the other in Hebrew: "Jonathan King". The most numerous have on one side the solar disc with eight rays, and on the other a ship's anchor in which it is possible to see an allusion to the conquest of Joppa (Jaffa) (*b*, the Greek inscription only is shown).

The two sons of Janneus quarrelled over the throne from 76–37, taking advantage in turn of foreign interventions. Hyrcanus II adopted the types of coins of his ancestors, with slight differences. Antigone Matathias endeavoured to follow a medium course, his coins bearing on the one side, in Greek: "Antigone King" and on the other in Hebrew "Matathias the High Priest and the community of the Jews" in which can be seen an anxiety to please the aristocracy of priests and doctors which would soon be known as the Sanhedrin. He often used the emblem of the double cornucopia and sometimes insignia of a more national character, such as the seven-branched candlestick of which this was the first representation.

HERODIAN DYNASTY

The dynasty of the Herods, Idumaeans partially assimilated to Judaism, was never national and did not seek to claim to to be so. All their inscriptions are in Greek.

Those of Herod the Great bear the inscription: "Herod King", but the emblems show a desire to respect Jewish scruples—the anchor, cornucopias, palms, flowers or fruit, in one instance the helmet and shield as evidence of a victorious campaign.

Archelaus and Antipas, his sons, followed the same principles. The former who reigned in Jerusalem from 4 B.C. to A.D. 6 displayed on the one side of the coin a plumed helmet, and on the other a bunch of grapes with the inscription: "Herod ethnarch" (*e*). The latter usually displayed on the one side a palm and the inscription "Herod tetrarch", on the other a laurel wreath and the inscription "Tiberiades".

The third brother, Philip, however, who reigned over a pagan territory on the confines of Syria and Palestine, did not scruple to put on his coins effigies of the emperor Augustus, and later of Tiberius.

The opportunism of the Herodian princes is fairly clearly shown by the monetary policy of Herod Agrippa. At first appointed king in the former tetrarchy of Philip, he followed the same custom and went as far as putting his own image on his coins (k): *Basileus Agrippas*. When, however, he received the whole of Palestine, he became more prudent. His most common coin bore on the one side three ears of corn, and on the other a canopy, a royal emblem, with the inscription: "King Agrippa" (l). At Caesarea, however, a coastal town which obtained its autonomy at that time, he had coins struck which were unmistakably pagan. Perhaps they should be related to the ceremonies of the year 44, in which this king met an unexpected death. In any case, it is not surprising that the devout should have looked upon it as a punishment from heaven (Acts 12. 19–23 sums up from a Christian point of view what is found in longer form in Flavius Josephus).

ROMAN RULERS

The Roman procurators, however, successors of Archelaus in his tetrarchy, and then of Agrippa in his kingdom, showed restraint. Their coins bore no compromising insignia but only the usual fertility emblems with the name of the reigning emperor (g, *Tiberiou Kaisar*). Silver coins were not always struck locally, denarii of a uniform type were used, with the imperial effigy and a Latin inscription (h): *Tiberius Cesar divi Augusti Filius Augustus*.

In the composite town of Caesarea, which had become autonomous under the emperor Claudius, the local coins assumed a pagan form. In this can be seen an image of the tension which was beginning to arise between Jews and Greeks

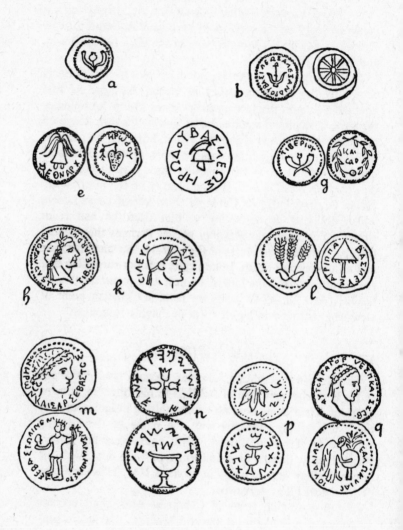

Fig. 56. Coins

in this town (*m*). The majority show on the one side the head of Nero and on the other the tutelary goddess of the town, crowned and leaning on a staff. The inscriptions are: Nerôn Kaisar Sebastos, "Nero Caesar Augustus", and Kaisaria hè pros to sebas to limeni, "Caesarea on the imperial sea".

THE JEWISH REVOLT

The revolt which broke out in 66 under Nero asserted the will to complete independence by striking for the first time a Jewish silver coin. Emblems inspired by the liturgy were adopted: the cup of the sabbatical repasts and three flowers. The old Phoenician characters were used which had, however, become obsolete (this detail can be verified by the funerary inscriptions: *n*. SHeQeL ISRa'EL, "shekel of Israel", and IeRWSHaLIM HaQaDASHaH, "Jerusalem the Holy"). The bronze coins have similar subjects and inscriptions: amphora of the feast of Tabernacles (cf. p. 55), baskets of the first fruits, branches and citron trees in connection with the feast (Levit. 23. 40), palms or vine leaves [*p*. (HeRuT) SIWN, "liberty of Sion", and ShaNat SheTaIM, "second year"].

The crushing of the revolt in 70 was the occasion of a special issue of imperial coins, known as "Judaea capta". One of them, at Caesarea, closed the series which interests us (*q*): on the one side the emperor Vespasian and "Autokrator Ves*pasianos* kai Sseb*astos*", "the emperor Vespasian Augustus", and on the other the figure of Victory writing on a shield suspended from a palm-tree and "Ioudaias ealokuias" "Judea captured".

THE GODS OF CANAAN AND THEIR IMAGES

The discovery at Ras-Shamra, the ancient Ugarit, of important mythological documents, together with various finds of the images of the gods, enables us to form an idea of the principal divinities of the Canaanite and Syrian pantheon, those whose memory the Bible has preserved for us.

Many others are only names for us, whether we come across them in a list of temples or see them mentioned in a man's name. It was, in fact, a constant habit in Semitic circles to form names of this kind and some have passed into European languages in translation—for instance: Natana El, "God gives" has become Theo-doros, Deo-datus, and Dieu-donné. Only the divinities of first rank, however, were sufficiently known for biblical writers to direct their polemics against them and it is these very gods about whom we have a fair amount of information.

ASHERA

In Mesopotamia from the earliest times figurines of baked clay have been found, representing an entirely naked woman,

[1] The following chapters are based on the interpretation of ancient picture documents. Several of them show rather involved scenes and it has been necessary to cut them or suppress useless details. At the same time every effort has been made to preserve the general lay-out

in forms sometimes crudely exaggerated. In Palestine, and the neighbouring countries, this fashion did not develop until the Middle Bronze Age onwards. It represents the goddess Ashera (fig. 57).

The most usual technique was to make these figurines in clay; the face was moulded, the back polished by hand. Sometimes the back was also moulded but the whole was again flattened (hence the name of figurine—plaques); sometimes bronze was used and economy of metal then led to elongated forms (fig. 57 b). The attitudes were varied: arms hanging (b), hands placed on the breast (e), sometimes each hand placed differently; often the figurine has flowers (d, f), sometimes a flower and a serpent (a). Some represent a woman obviously pregnant (g). The figures representing a woman suckling a child in all probability do not belong to the same iconographical cycle; many of them are seated or else partially clothed—in any case they are not very numerous. The head-dresses are likewise varied. The bronzes usually show the high tiara with horns of the deities of Mesopotamia and Syria (b); many figures of baked clay have the two S-shaped curls, emblem of the great Egyptian goddess Hathor (f), others have the cylindrical crown of the goddesses and queens of Syria in the Late Bronze Age (d, e), others again the ordinary women's head-dress (g). There is no correlation between the different types of attitude or head-dress, and it must be admitted that all these images belong to the same iconographical cycle, with variants due to times and places. It can be observed, however, that the mythological attributes, tiara with horns, Hathoric curls, cylindrical crown, become less frequent in the Iron Ages. This seems to correspond to the arrival of a population which was no longer interested in the old myths and only kept up their cultus in the form of a superstition. Certain of these figurines were perhaps nothing more than charms—(g) for instance, which is from Iron Age II

Likewise in the Iron Age appeared pillar figurines entirely without mythological attributes (c, h); they seem to have originated from northern Syria and their diffusion would denote an indirect influence of the Arameans. The lower part of the body is replaced by a kind of hollow cylinder made on the potter's wheel, breast and arms were traced out by hand, the head sometimes treated in the same way (c), or else moulded with a certain amount of skill (h).

No one has any doubt but that these figurines represent a mother-goddess. Egyptian representations enable us to be explicit. The people of the Delta, in fact, adopted certain deities of Canaan in the course of the Late Bronze Age, eighteenth–nineteenth dynasties. One stele represents the goddess wearing the curls and lunar crescent of Hathor (a); she

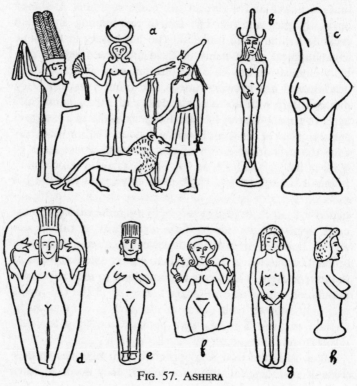

FIG. 57. ASHERA

is standing on a lion, a probable borrowing from the iconography of Anatolia or Upper Mesopotamia, designating a
goddess of the first rank; in her right hand she holds flowers
which she is presenting to the Egyptian fertility god Min,
and in her left hand, the unfavourable side, serpents which
she presents to the Canaanite god Réshef, closely associated
with the idea of death. The meaning of this imagery would
seem to be that the goddess gives birth equally to all things,
good or bad, and assigns them to each of the gods, according
to his particular character. On a figure similar to that just
described is found the inscription: "Quadesh ('the Holy One'),
lady of heaven and mistress of all the gods". In the Ugaritic
documents, the deity which corresponds most closely to this
description is Ashera, spouse of the great god El, mother of
the gods and sometimes of monsters, and although there is
no absolutely formal reason for making the identification, the
best specialists do not hesitate to admit it.

Now the Bible makes numerous allusions to the worship
of Ashera which continued to flourish until the exile, despite
the reproaches of the prophets and law-givers. It is extremely
probable that the "queen of heaven" whom women honoured
was none other (Jerem. 44. 17, see also 3 Kings 15. 13, 16. 33;
4 Kings 21. 7).

As will be explained a little further on, this divinity fell into
neglect after the exile and it is to the point that the Greek
version interprets "Ashera" by "tree or sacred wood", and
many moderns by "stakes or sacred post". According to the
biblical expressions, the Israelite Ashera must have been a
wooden log planted in the earth and to some degree fashioned
after the manner of the pillar figurines, and it was sometimes
decorated with fabrics (4 Kings 23. 7).

ISHTAR

In the Ugaritic myths the goddess Ishtar (in Greek Astarte)
plays only a subordinate rôle as associate of the god *Baal*.

She is often called "Ishtar-name-of-Baal", which seems to signify that she introduced his adorers into the near presence of the god, as, according to Semitic ideas, the name gives access to the person. This view can be illustrated by a stele discovered in the land of Moab (fig. 58 e) on which may be seen on the left the local Baal (perhaps already Kemosh, Jerem. 48. 13), on the right his Ishtar effaces herself after having brought in an adorer. The god is wearing the crown of the Pharaohs and the sceptre of the gods of Egypt, the goddess has a tiara decorated with ostrich plumes, an Egyptian divine insignia, and the *crux ansata,* the sign of life. The adorer is wearing a folded Egyptian tunic with the national head-band of the men of the desert, he is thus a nomad chieftain of high rank. The iconographical tradition is that of the Late Bronze period, but the monument itself could be somewhat later. Egyptian influence is common throughout Palestine.

In Mesopotamia, however, Ishtar had a much richer personality. Goddess of fecundity, she was also goddess of war. From Assyria the image of Ishtar the warrior was introduced into Upper Syria as early as the Iron Age (g). Despite its origin the stiffness of this image bears witness to the local style. Mounted on a lioness the goddess is wearing the cylindrical fluted crown, surmounted by an astral disc which identifies her with the planet Venus; she is armed with a sword, with two bows in their cases (above the shoulders) and with a quiver from which the winged arrows can be seen emerging.

With the spread of Mesopotamian influence at the time of the great empires, the cult of Ishtar extended throughout the coastal region. Phoenician inscriptions of the Persian and Hellenistic epoch make reference to it. It was then that the memory of the ancient Ashera was lost. Figurines of the mother-goddess, sometimes traditional, sometimes Hellenistic, continued to be made, but we cannot enter here into Greco-oriental mythology which is very complex and would not be useful for an understanding of the Bible. Thus it is not surprising that archaeologists have often called the plaques and figurines described above Astarte, but this appellation is only exact for the early periods.

ANAT

In ancient mythology the really active goddess was Anat, a warrior virgin knowing nothing of love and a friend of slaughter. On more than one occasion her fury saved her brother Baal in a difficult predicament, and it was sometimes he who had to intervene to force her to spare human beings. Several documents attribute the power of flight to her. Thus she can be recognized on Syrian cylinders representing a very young goddess armed and winged (*d*) or playing with the wild beasts which she hunts and tames (*b*). Anat was also adopted by the Egyptians of the Late Bronze Age. She had been popular in Palestine, if we are to judge by the place names in which her name occurs, "Bet-Anat" and "Anatot", but she was forgotten at the time when the biblical books were cast in their final form: it is highly probable that she was early replaced by the female warrior Ishtar.

EL

In the Ugaritic myths, the supreme god is El, the "father of the gods" and "creator of things". His great age, his moral and metaphysical character, the remoteness of his dwelling on the confines of the sky and the ocean, lessened his interest in simple humans; thus it is rare to find an image which represents him with certainty. He may, however, be recognized on a Ugaritic stele which shows a god seated on a throne, wearing a Mesopotamian horned tiara to which the ostrich plumes of Egypt have been added, with full-flowing beard and wearing the tunic and mantle; in front of him a king or priest makes a gesture of adoration (fig. 58 *a*).

RESHEF

Reference has been made to the Canaanite god Reshef whom the Egyptians have identified with the wicked Seth, the enemy of Osiris. They like to represent him as an angry warrior, heavily armed and dressed in the Asiatic manner (fig. 58 c). As usual, his bonnet is decorated with the head of a horned animal, perhaps the horned viper rather than the gazelle as has often been thought. Numerous bronze figurines, representing warrior gods, could doubtless be attributed to him, but none of them bears this attribute, the Semitic model of which we still lack.

BAAL

The name of Baal, which simply means "master", has covered various mythical personalities. The Ugaritic documents, however, attribute it solely to Hadad, god of the storm, the rain, and thus of fertility. He has been likened to a bull, of whom the thunder is his bellow and the lightning the stroke of his horn. A curious myth of the death and revival of Baal must have some connection with the alternation of the seasons. A series of other myths attributes to him the rôle of a demiurge when he kills the sea dragon Yam. Others again tell of his connection with royalty consigning his father El to some extent to the sphere of oblivion. In fact, outside the Israelite milieu in which the personality of El has been definitely purified, it is Baal who everywhere won first place in worship. He can be recognized in the image of a god, young indeed, but already majestic, who moves forward with resolution, holding a mace in his right hand and in the left a spear with which he strikes the ground, the handle of which branches out into lightning (fig. 58, f).

FIG. 58. SYRIAN AND CANAANITE GODS

MOUNTED GODS

Reference has been made to the custom of representing the gods standing upon an animal. It is of Anatolian origin and spread over Upper Syria and in Assyria. Up to the present, however, no example is known in any coastal country. In the beginning the animal as much as the human figure represented the personality of the god. In a more nuanced imagery the animal is held by the god by means of a kind of halter and thus reduced to the rôle of mount. This is the case for Ishtar as we have seen, as well as for the Syrian Hadad (fig. 58, h). It has thus been suggested that the golden calves of Jeroboam should be understood as the steeds of Yahweh and not as his image (3 Kings 12. 28). It is certain that the explanation must be sought in this direction, the cultus of the Egyptian bull, Apis, having spread much later; it is certain, too, that no other example of sacred bulls represented alone is known. The initiative of Jeroboam would thus have made it possible to indicate the divine presence without making a divine image properly so-called, thus respecting the letter of the Decalogue. This, however, was too subtle for the people not to be misled by it, and in any event the Israelite conscience could not admit the assimilation of Yahweh to Hadad.

CHAPTER VIII

CLOTHES, WEAPONS, MUSICAL INSTRUMENTS

THE PATRIARCHS' CONTEMPORARIES

A well-known Egyptian painting shows us Asiatics contemporary with the Patriarchs (fig. 60). It is to be seen at Beni-Hassan in the tomb of a government servant, one of whose functions was to control the entry of nomads into the Delta. There armed men, and women with their children and their donkeys, can be seen. All are dressed in materials which are woven or embroidered with bright colours in which blue and red predominate, and which the artist has represented flat according to a fairly general convention. The women are uniformly wearing a draped garment passing under the right arm and over the left shoulder (*h*), the men wear the same garment or a simple loin-cloth. All are bareheaded. The men are wearing thonged sandals, the women small, soft boots, the tradition of which was still in existence about fifty years ago.

The draped garment is best represented on Palestinian scarabs of the Hykos period, coming from the Asiatics themselves and somewhat later than the painting of Beni-Hassan. Two men can be seen wrapped in a mantle with one or two folds (*j, m*), another is wearing a loin-cloth, a woman already

 has the straight tunic with some embroidery which will be found later (*l*). The mantle was fastened by a strong pin with an eyelet hole through which a string was passed—one of them has been discovered on a garment in a tomb (fig. 59).

FIG. 59

The weapons are: the spear; the double-curved bow made of pieces of wood skilfully adjusted and accompanied by a quiver (e), the axe with curved handle (e, blade near the hand), and a kind of sabre the blade of which was made convex by hammering (c). Diggings have also produced numerous daggers.

One man is playing the lyre (f) and is carrying on his back a wineskin or bag.

It is generally considered that one of the donkeys is carrying a bellows of folded leather (g, above). It would thus represent a group of travelling artisans plying various trades, to be found curiously enough in the story of the sons of Cain, one a musician, the other a metallurgist. In Arabic, "Cain" means "blacksmith" (Gen. 4. 20–22). The Egyptian inscription, however, merely speaks of trading in spices and perfumes (Gen. 43. 11). The other donkey is carrying baskets made of esparto grass, with two small children.

LATE BRONZE

The Late Bronze period has left us numerous representations. Both dress and the whole setting of life had become enriched and complicated and the documents provide evidence of the type of art to which the peoples of the coast had attained (fig. 61).

In the upper classes of society, the principal garment both for men and women was a long tunic, embroidered with geometrical designs—circles or ladders. Over this the men of the highest rank wore a mantle fastened on the left shoulder (a, e), and the women a second tunic, wider and shorter than the first (a). Men of a slightly lower rank kept the national draped cloak, wound several times around the body (c). For hunting and hand to hand combat the tunic was short and ornamented with diagonal embroidery. The ordinary people wore only a loin-cloth. A queen would wear a toque with a flat foundation, but her servant-maid went bare-headed. Men

FIG. 60. ANCIENT NOMADS

FIG. 61. CANAANITES

often had the head shaved, but it seems they sometimes wore a wig. The rank and file soldiers kept their hair (*d, e*). We do not know the precise meaning of these differences. Footwear is not represented.

The elegance of certain gestures should be noted: a queen presents a flower to the king with one hand and with the other holds a napkin under his goblet, so that there is no risk of even a drop of liquid soiling the royal garments (the other end of the napkin hangs over the queen's shoulder). A female singer, her mouth wide open, accompanies herself on the lyre, while tame partridges flutter around the throne or peck the ground. In this mixture of courtesy and familiarity, there is something which recalls the best moments of our Middle Ages.

The weapons still comprise: the spear to which a round or rectangular shield is sometimes added; the bow and the quiver (in a case attached to the chariot, *e*), the dagger and short sword (*b*, the hunter on the left grasps the lion's paw with one hand and drives a dagger in his flank with the other); the former sabre has acquired a more handsome if not more useful shape, in which can be recognized the *harpè* of the tales of the Greek heroes, ordinarily designated under this name (*e*, on the right). The excavations sometimes show the remains of a tunic covered with scales of bronze, but this is not shown in the local documents and must have been rare.

IRON AGE

After the fall of the Canaanite civilization, the first centuries of the Iron Age have left us very few illustrated documents. The only important collection comes from Tell Halaf in Upper Syria (cf. p. 50). One of the scenes represented provides a perfect illustration of a biblical passage (fig. 63, *a* and *b*, 2 Kings 2. 15–16: "Come forward they did, twelve men that acknowledged Isboseth as the heir of Saul, and twelve followers of David, and met one another. Each caught his man by the head and thrust his sword deep"). It may thus be admitted that these illustrations provide a good representation of the common customs of the peoples of Syria and Palestine around the tenth century.

The men are still wearing the loin-cloth, some have a long tunic decorated with fringe and held in position by a belt. The hair and beard are still intact, the majority of the men are bare-headed but a young man is wearing a bonnet, the point of which falls over to the back (c). A king is still wearing the draped garment wound round once in the Mesopotamian fashion (h). His crown, apparently made of plaques of metal, has a cavity which must have been used for inserting a precious stone (2 Kings 12. 30); the curved stick he is holding against his shoulder is perhaps the ancient sceptre of the

nomad chieftains which the Egyptians have made known to us.

A woman is only distinguishable from the men by her long, wavy hair, and the rings she wears on her ankles (f). A queen,

FIG. 62

seated, has the royal crown and a double-row collar of beads (g).

Garments were no longer fastened by means of pins but of fibulae or buckles (fig. 62), the use of which continued down to the Middle Ages.

As has already been said when discussing the pottery, it is impossible to make a clean cut between the First and Second Iron Ages. In the Syrian ivories found in the Assyrian treasure of Nimrod (ancient Kalakh), the art is finer than in the basalts of Tell Halaf, but they relate to the same period.

An example is the head of a crowned woman wearing two curls which pass in front of the ears, a necklace with two rows of pearls and a row of pendants (fig. 64 b). A typical scene shows a queen seated on a throne adorned with inlaid work: her costume and head-dress are practically the same as those already described (fig. 64 h). The servants and musicians who surround her have a straight gown with a few embroidery

FIG. 63. ARAMEANS

decorations on the belt, one of them is playing the double oboe. A dancer is wearing a short tunic and accompanies himself with an instrument in a rectangular frame difficult to identify (*f*).

An Ammonite statuette, artistically mediocre but very rich in details, shows a king or a dignitary (*e*). The beard is intact as is the hair kept in place by a band; four small curls in front of the ears can be seen—Leviticus forbade the Jews to cut them (19. 27, 21. 5), thus certain devout sects have continued to use them down to the present day. The statuette is wearing a pleated tunic held in place by a long waistband whose embroidered ends fall below the knees. The draped garment has been reduced to a scarf wound round waist and shoulders, one corner falling in the centre of the back.

Examples, dated with far greater certainty, come from an Assyrian treasure found in Upper Egypt, one of them bearing the inscription: "for Hazael, our master". Thus they come from the workshops of Damascus about 845 B.C. (4 Kings 8. 7–15). The elegance of the Phoenician style counterbalances a certain stiffness found in the pieces of Syrian origin (cf. figs. 34 and 35, of the same origin); this is a new zenith of the local art. A king is wearing the simple tunic, decorated only with fringe at the foot, and the garment draped as a scarf. He has on his feet sandals with quarterings (fig. 64 *d*). A woman's head shows the hair style with large curls common in the coastal countries and on top a small square of embroidered material, trimmed with pendants and two ear-rings (*a*).

Among the weapons of Tell Halaf we again find the straight sword (fig. 63 *a*), the spear, the bow. The introduction of iron led to the abandonment of the *harpè*. The sling, however, is once again in honour (*e*). The king has a long straight sword which presupposes good use of the resources of the new metal (*h*, at the side of the figure). A little later it would become general. Several figures are wearing the conical helmet and one of them seems to be represented with a complete coat of mail (*d*, spear and shield in very poor condition).

ASSYRIAN DOCUMENTS

It is from Assyrian documents that we derive information as to the dress and equipment of the peoples of the seventh and eighth centuries, the final part of the Iron Age. They show us primarily that there was no difference between the Israelites and the other Syrian nations, which justifies the method we have so far followed. The Assyrian artists, however, make a clear distinction between foreigners and their own compatriots and they cannot be suspected of having used conventional designs.

FIG. 64. ARAMEANS

These documents show several innovations. The man of a certain rank, those for instance who carry the tribute of Jehu, King of Israel, to Salmanasar III, have the mantle fastened on the shoulder and trimmed with fringe. Where the tradition had been preserved since Canaanite times is not known (fig. 65, b, the figure on the right shows the shoulders front view and the rest of the body in profile); the same men have the bonnet with a falling point, and small boots with turned up toes. The common people, such as the deportees of Lachis (4 Kings 18. 17), have a head-band the ends of which droop on to the cheeks which are often shaved, the short-sleeved tunic and the loin-cloth inherited from preceding epochs. The women, and the girls even when quite small, have a long veil which covers the head and hangs down to the heels (fig. 65 c). Certain local figurines confirm these head-dresses, but they are too rough to give any details and are not worth reproduction.

The defenders of Lachis have the traditional projectile weapons, but their tall pointed helmets represent a more modern style (fig. 65 a). Their large round shields are fixed to the rubble-work of the tower they are defending. Moreover, the documentation as a whole shows that weapons had not developed perceptibly since the period of Tell Halaf, in particular the two types of sword are still found: the one, short and broad, is that of the foot soldiers, the other and longer is reserved for the mounted soldiery.

PHOENICIA

It is from Phoenicia that the best documents on dress in the time of the Persian and Macedonian empires have come down to us. There we find that the Greek influence was prior to the conquest of Alexander, but that it never completely eliminated local customs.

It was more usual for the Persians to adopt the costume of their subject peoples than to give them their own. Nevertheless people gladly imitated the ample bell-shaped rider's cloak fitted with a hood. Figurines of the "Persian horseman" are frequent. In Hellenistic times this was one of the representations of Horus as a child (fig. 66, *c*). This garment can be seen on the child (*h*) and it is probable that the wearing of it never fell into disuse. Persian influence is also to be seen in figurines of hooded men. The one here shown (fig. 66, *b*) is pulling at his beard as a sign of mourning (Esdras 9. 3).

Full dress costume in Persian times can be seen from a

FIG. 65. ASSYRIAN DOCUMENTS

representation of a king of Byblos in adoration before the Great Goddess of his city (*d*). He has a toque with a flat foundation from which two ribbons hang down and a shawl folded triangularly. It was to a garment of this kind that was most easily applied a law of Deuteronomy (22. 12)[1] which was still in force in Gospel times (Matt. 9. 20, 23. 5). The king is wearing the full beard which the Jews retained and which many of them still keep. It can be seen that this people had made into a distinctive mark of nationality what had originally been a common practice or a simple mark of seemliness.

Phoenician funeral steles show us the dress of well-to-do people (*a*). They have a small bonnet with a flat foundation, the beard is often shaved off and the tunic "without seam" can be distinctly seen (cf. John 19. 23). It was made of two rectangular-shaped pieces of material sewn together over the shoulders and the sides without having been cut. Sufficient opening for head and hands was provided and the proportions were sufficiently ample for a kind of half-sleeve to form of itself without adjustment. A girdle kept all in place and gave different draped effects. On the example given here the braid which borders the seams and makes it possible to follow their line can be seen; all the fullness of the skirt is brought round to the front. It is known from the Rabbinical documents that the tunic of the Jewish High Priests was made of a single length of material hanging down before and behind and sewn together at the sides, with an opening for the head.

Outer garments, tunics or even cloaks open from top to bottom were made on the same principle (*e*); in Phoenician circles this garment seems to have been reserved for certain acts of worship.

In the fields, workers had a tunic with short, close-fitting sleeves, more or less gathered up into a belt (*g*). For harder work, or on the water, a loin-cloth was considered sufficient.

---

[1]"Thou shalt wear tasselled strings at the four corners of the garment thou wearest."

FIG. 66. HELLENIZED PHOENICIANS

Boys were often represented naked or wearing a mantle only. On other occasions they are shown with a short straight tunic.

All the figures of women are of the Hellenistic period, they show that Greek forms of dress had spread without encountering opposition: the pleated robe, with or without sleeves, and large shawl, or *himation*, placed on the head and draped elegantly around the body (*k, m*). In principle this garment was in no way different from these shown us in the Assyrian documents. No text leads us to think that Jewish women were dressed differently from other women of their time and there are no grounds for supposing this. Small girls were dressed exactly as their elders (*j*). A woman half covered with a sack (*o*) is doubtless a mourner or else a bearer of offerings in the funeral cultus of Adonis. This use is well attested by other documents and the Bible makes several allusions to it (Isaias 32. 10–12).

Several figurines of schoolboys show us how the diptychs or writing-tablets were used: one of the two boards was placed on the knees, while the other hung down in front (*f*, schoolboy wearing a *himation*). In practice any practically flat object was used for writing, and often pottery shards.

The figurines here reproduced (*b, c, e–o*) were discovered recently at Kharayeb in the Lebanon and provide a good example of the local art. While they have neither the elegance nor the finish of their Hellenistic models, they show a good grasp of the movement of the latter. They have succeeded in being distinctive and are evidence of the profound hellenization of popular taste in the milieu from which they have issued.

MODERN DRESS IN PALESTINE

A few details about the modern costume of the Arabs in Palestine will perhaps be appreciated. The men wear on their heads a square of light weight material, the *keffiyeh*, held in place by a band made of goats' hair, the *agal*. We have already pointed out that Egyptian drawings of the second millennium portray people from the desert wearing the same sort of head-dress made of the same features, although differently arranged. It would thus seem that the style is truly national, but no further trace of it is found in the iconography of the following centuries and in modern times it has reappeared only in the case of the nomad camel-drivers; its adoption by the generality of the sedentary population is recent. The gown open in front, crossed over then held in place by a loop, called the *qumbass*, must come from medieval Persia, the miniatures of which often show similar garments. The wide-seated breeches, *serual*, are also of Iranian origin, but earlier; they were worn by the Persians and by the Parthian and Iranian horsemen. The use of these, like that of other parts of their costume, must have spread in the third and fourth centuries of the Christian era. The bedouin cloak, the *abaye*, is made like the garments "without seam" described above.

The relative remoteness of Palestine and its isolation in the ancient Turkish empire have preserved there an archaic feminine costume which is no longer seen in neighbouring Arab countries. Beneath the Byzantine style the pre-exilic tradition can be seen, with its straight gown, and a head veil that does not hide the face. The embroideries with which it is adorned seem only to have become general since the eighteenth century of our era. A few years ago they were uniformly red in colour, of a fairly plain design, recalling the well-known style of the ancient Turkish countries of Europe. The final stage of an ancient Byzantine style can be seen there, but the present tendency is towards something more decorative.

All things considered, the appearance of the Arab population of Palestine differs considerably from what that of the peoples of the New Testament must have been. The artists who in representing the latter have derived their inspiration from classical models were nearer the truth than those who thought they should reproduce what they saw in the country.

CHAPTER IX

TOOLS

FLINT TOOLS

The tools found in the excavation of ancient sites are less numerous by far than the weapons, and, with the single exception of Egypt, tools are very seldom found illustrated. Thus our information on this point which is, however, of primary importance, is meagre. Yet it has been possible to find here and there certain evidences of an evolution which was, indeed, slow.

In the first place it must be pointed out that stone tools remained in use long after the invention of metal work. If the last flint arrows disappeared before the time at which this study begins, flint sickles were in use throughout the whole of the Bronze Age, and often enough we find toothed blades that were once fixed in a curved frame of wood, bone or horn. The principal advantage of the discovery of iron was primarily its economy rather than its sharp-cutting quality, for it was a long time before its technique was mastered. During the Iron Age, flint tools disappeared.

HANDLES

The improvement of technique can be recognized in the fitting of the tools with handles.

In the case of thin parts the solution was found immediately: the blade was extended by a prong which penetrated into the handle and was held in place by rivets (fig. 67, knife *d,* sickles *b* and *c,* goad *h*). The shapes of these pieces of iron were already known in the Bronze Age. This was also the usual form of handle for swords, daggers, javelins and arrows.

What is more surprising for us is that for a long time a similar method continued to be in use for heavy tools. In the Bronze Ages, the axe for tool-making was a thick blade inserted into the handle. This was inherited from prehistoric tradition when the stone tool could not be fixed otherwise. At the most, advantage was taken of the ease of shaping a metal axe so that it did not tend to penetrate too far into the wood; but axes with a socket or with a handle hole were reserved for armament. During Iron Age I, the difficulty of working the new metal led to the retention of these archaic forms of which axe (*m*) is an example already considerably developed; the hole which pierces the flange and through which a rivet or a link can pass is a rare improvement. Pieces of this kind can be considered indifferently as axes, large chisels or adzes. In the latter case they had to be fixed to the handle through the intermediary of a second piece of wood in accordance with a method with which ethnography has made us familiar (*y*).

A second method of fitting a handle is the socket, in which the flattened metal is folded cylindrically around the handle. This was early used for lances and javelins. Later, and perhaps not until after the exile, carpenters' chisels were made in bronze and also in iron, arranged in this way (*f*). From the Herodian period we have a hoe with rectangular horizontal blade with a right-angled socket so that the handle can be fitted directly into the tool; already this is the same system used by gardeners today.

The ploughshares, in bronze or in iron, were small points which a kind of improvised socket fixed to the end of a thick stick (*l*). These ploughs thus scratched the earth without turning it over. From the Iron Age onwards there were hoes with a socket (*g*) fixed to the handle by an intermediary piece like the adzes.

The assembly of heavy tools by means of a handle hole was

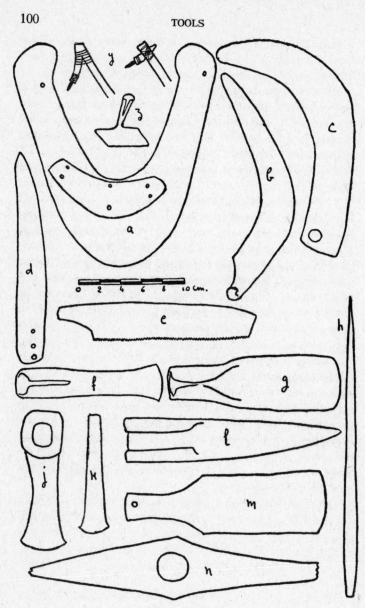

FIG. 67. TOOLS

difficult to carry out in iron. It was not until the end of Iron Age I, thus towards the middle of the time of the Kings, that this began to be seen on the pick (n), found in the same stratum as the axe (m) and thus contemporary with it. The process developed and, in the Hellenistic period, axes, adzes (j), and various double-instruments (pick-axe, etc.) were found. It may be considered that at that time, but not earlier, the quality of the tools had caught up with that of the weapons and that all the resources of the blacksmith's art were used on them.

The date that should be assigned to a piece of iron strengthening a wooden spade cannot be accurately determined. It was probably later than the Exile (a, specimen repaired in ancient times).

A bronze saw (e) has been found, but clearly we cannot expect that an iron saw should be sufficiently well preserved to be recognizable. Various small tools, such as awls or borers, are also found in fairly considerable quantity.

The biblical texts do not invite us to reach for a greater variety of types (1 Kings 13. 20 and 2 Kings 12. 31; the vocabulary is often difficult).

The poor quality of the tools in comparison with the extent and beauty of the results obtained is for us one of the most astonishing features in ancient civilizations. It must be supposed that people made up for the poor quality by a great expenditure of time and fatigue.

CHAPTER X

THE MEANS OF TRANSPORT

It must be recalled in the first place that the oldest means of transport known is a man's back and, astonishing as that may seem, the archives of the kingdom of Mari which flourished around 1800 on the Middle Euphrates show that caravans of bearers were still sometimes employed for long journeys across the desert (cf. 3 Kings 5. 15). But donkeys were preferred as stronger and easier to feed, and down to our own times they have remained the favourite means of transport of the farmer or of the humble oriental nomad (fig. 60 *g*).

WAGGONS

According to the same texts ox-drawn waggons were used for heavy transport, for instance for bringing timber from the coastal region to the Euphrates. These waggons are represented but rarely. According to the Egyptian artists, they served the "Peoples of the Sea" who came from the coasts of Palestine. The waggons were small boxes with full wheels. They are

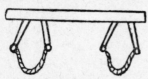

FIG. 68

found again in Assyrian deportation scenes: the wheels were fitted with spokes, the box, still small, was partly lattice work, the yoke was placed on the withers of the oxen and fixed by two V-shaped rods and a rather loose rope (figs. 65 and 68). It is still the mode of harnessing used in the East. The Bible sometimes mentions this kind of vehicle (Gen. 45. 19–27; Num. 7. 3; 1 Kings 6. 7; 2 Kings 6. 3).

CHARIOTS

The same Mari texts very frequently mention the use of chariots drawn by horses. As they were used for war and on royal parades, representations of them are numerous, both in Egyptian art and in that of the Canaanites of the Late Bronze Age or of the Aramaeans of Tell Halaf, the Assyrians or the later empires. The model of the ancient chariot, moreover, has only evolved in tiny details: it is a light box carried on two small wheels with spokes. It is drawn by two horses harnessed to a curved pole which is fastened to the bottom of the body and which a rod links up with the upper edge (fig. 69, a).

Judging by the examples found in the royal Egyptian tombs the box had a wooden framework and sides of thick material or of leather, esparto or wicker-work. From a very reliable literary text we learn that they knew how to cover the chariot with a hood for the journey, but no illustration shows this. The pole rested on the withers of the horses by means of a yoke attached to the neck by a rather complicated system of straps (fig. 61, e). It was impossible, however, to avoid pressing on the horse's throat, which prevented him from giving all his strength. They did, however, try to remedy this inconvenience by means of padding which the Assyrians still use. To avoid any risk of overturning backwards, the wheels were always placed at the back of the box. Despite these precautions, the transport capacity of the ancient chariots were always slight as Commandant Lefebvre des Noëttes has shown in his book, now become a classic.

During racing and sometimes at the hunt, the chariot was mounted by a single man. For war or a more dangerous hunt, the master of the chariot reserved the shooting with the bow for himself and a driver took charge of the horses (fig. 69, a). The Assyrians, following an ancient custom, Anatolian in origin, added to their crew a third and fourth man. Several biblical texts also mention these "equerries" (literally "third").

HORSE AND CAMEL RIDING

The riding of horses is also mentioned in a Mari document. Perhaps, however, it was only a sport or a means of breaking horses in for in the Bronze Age it only figured in a very small number of Egyptian designs difficult to interpret. It is at Tell Halaf that we see horsemen armed for war for the first time. They have the conical helmet and round shield, and hold a

FIG. 69. MEANS OF TRANSPORT

weapon of which it is impossible to say whether it is a lance or a long straight sword (fig. 69, b).

The same representations also show us for the first time a harnessed and mounted camel (fig. 69, c). The man is seated on a pack-saddle or sack of wool, which covers the animal's hump. This position would not allow him to withstand the jolts which the camel gives with its quick pace. It was not until the eighth century that Assyrian art showed Arabs fighting from the top of their camels, but since it is always true that illustrated documents are later than the literary texts, we can recognize in the account of the Madianite invasion the first document on the arrival of camel-drivers in the coastal region of Palestine (Judges 6–8).

It was at the time of the Persian, Greek and Roman-Byzantine Empires that the Arab camel-drivers began to enter the arable lands of Syria in large numbers, whether for their own migration or to serve in transport. Their presence contributed to limit the development of wheeled vehicles which a big draught animal easily replaced. If the Roman-Byzantine Empire established a close network of routes and services of vehicles, this was the application of general measures which had not perhaps sufficient justification in particular circumstances. The Arab empires abandoned them. This was again one of the cases in which the "picturesque Orient", which so impressed the travellers in the last century, does not go back to remote antiquity and gives a false picture of biblical times.

SHIPS

The ancient Israelites were never sailors. If the coastal tribes served on the Canaanite ships, they did not communicate the liking for navigation to the rest (Gen. 49. 13; Deut. 33. 18; Judges 5. 17). In later literature, fear rather than familiarity with the things of the sea is found (Jonas 1, Psalm 106. 23). Ezechiel describing the ship of Tyre (27) has probably mixed the characteristics of two very different types: a fighting galley with a small auxiliary sail, and a heavy cargo boat driven along by a single large sail. These Phoenician ships were very similar to those the Greeks constructed and little, moreover, is known of their details.

FIG. 70. PHOENICIAN SHIP OF ROMAN ERA

The Greek cargo ship continued to develop until the Roman era. A sarcophagus found near Sidon gives a representation of it which compares favourably with those found in Italy and may be considered as reliable (fig. 70).

The vessel is empty and the smooth hull is only partially submerged. It can be seen that the keel is not prolonged by a drop-keel. The stem is continued by a sort of beak which carries a crow's nest where a look-out man can be posted. The poop is prolonged by an elegant swan's neck and carries a gangway for manœuvres. It is well designed to rise with the movement of the waves. The boat is thus heavy in front and light in the stern, made to run before the sea and not to fight against it. The superstructure with its projecting surround is open at the rear to allow the control oars to pass, one on each side. Whatever the precautions taken, this was a weak point. Under the right corner of the sail can be seen the roof of a cabin which did not occupy the full width. The ship was decked at least in part, for the heads of the transverse beams can be seen projecting, but, according to other documents, they must have been placed in a lower position. Various ancient authors confirm the Acts of the Apostles and say that in the case of a storm the framework was strengthened by binding it with rope. It is probable that it was weak and badly put together.

According to the first findings of underseas archaeology, it is thought that a ship of this kind might have been about thirty yards long or a little over. In this case, it is probable that our artist has reduced the length in relation to the spread of the sail and the height of the hull.

The most serious defect in these ancient ships was their system of sails, which did not allow any fine seamanship. It was reduced to one large, heavy square sail and it is not known whether it was possible to shorten it in case of bad weather. An innovation at the time was the spare or "mizzen" sail placed in front. Concealed and almost useless for normal sailing, it must have been used chiefly in the case of a storm to keep the boat in the direction of the wind, and thus back to the waves, the large sail then being hauled down (Acts 27. 40). If there was danger of being carried too far, they preferred to throw into the sea a floating anchor, a kind of raft made to control the movement and not to give the wind free play. Attached to the poop it kept the ship head on to wind and sea, thus preventing the boat from falling athwart and capsizing (Acts 27. 17).

With such sails and no keel, it was impossible to come round the wind. This was particularly troublesome when leaving the coast of Syria to sail westwards, for during the whole of the fine season it is precisely from that quarter that the wind comes. They were reduced to keeping close to the coast, by taking advantage of the land breeze which blows in the early morning (Acts 27. 4–8).

On this ship St Paul, as in other times Abraham on his donkey, left the land of his fathers, and carried the promises of God to distant parts.

SELECT BIBLIOGRAPHY

In this series:

DANIEL-ROPS: *What is the Bible?*

GÉLIN, Albert: *The Religion of Israel.*

STEINMANN, Jean: *Biblical Criticism.*

ALBRIGHT, W. F.: *The Archaeology of Palestine,* Harmondsworth and Baltimore, Penguin Books, 1956.

BURROWS, Millar: *What Mean These Stones?* New Haven, Conn., American Schools of Oriental Research, 1941.

CROWFOOT, J. W., and others: *Early Ivories From Samaria,* London, Palestine Exploration Fund, 1938; *The Buildings at Samaria,* London, Palestine Exploration Fund, 1942.

GARROD, Dorothy, and others: *The Stone Age of Mount Carmel,* London and New York, Oxford Univ. Press, 1937.

GARSTANG, John, and GARSTANG, J. B. E.: *The Story of Jericho,* London, Marshall, Morgan and Scott, 1948.

GLUECK, Nelson: *The Other Side of the Jordan,* New Haven, Conn., American Schools of Oriental Research, 1945; *The River Jordan,* London, Lutterworth Press, and Philadelphia, Pa, Westminster Press, 1946.

GROLLENBERG, L. H.: *Atlas of the Bible,* translated and edited by H. H. Rowley and J. M. H. Reid, London and New York, Nelson, 1956.

GUY, P. L. O., and ENGBERG, R. M.: *Megiddo Tombs,* Cambridge, Cambridge Univ. Press, and Chicago, Chicago Univ. Press, 1938.

KENYON, Kathleen M.: *Beginning in Archaeology,* London, Phoenix House, and New York, Praeger, 1952.

LOUD, Gordon: *Megiddo Ivories,* Chicago, Chicago Univ. Press, 1939, and Cambridge, Cambridge Univ. Press, 1940.

MACALISTER, R. A. S.: *The Excavation of Gezer,* 3 vols., London, John Murray, 1912.

MACDONALD, E.: *Beth-Pelet II,* London, Bernard Quaritch, 1932.

PRITCHARD, J. B.: *The Ancient Near East in Pictures Relating to the Old Testament*, London, Oxford Univ. Press, and Princeton, N.J., Princeton Univ. Press, 1955.

REISNER, G. A., and others: *Harvard Excavations at Samaria, 1908–1910*, London, Oxford Univ. Press, and Cambridge, Mass., Harvard Univ. Press.

ROWE, Alan: *The Topography and History of Beth-Shan* (Publications of the Palestine section of the Museum of Pennsylvania, vol. I), Philadelphia, Pa, Philadelphia Univ. Press, 1930; *The Four Canaanite Temples* (vol. II, same series), Philadelphia, Pa, Philadelphia Univ. Press, 1940.

SIMONS, J., S.J.: *Jerusalem in the Old Testament*, Leiden, Brill, 1952.

SUKENIK, E. L.: *Ancient Synagogues in Palestine and Greece*, London, Oxford Univ. Press, 1934.

SUTCLIFFE, Edmund F., S.J.: *The Monks of Qumran*, London, Burns and Oates, and Westminster, Md, The Newman Press, 1960.

WRIGHT, G. E., and FILSON, F. V.: *The Westminster Historical Atlas to the Bible*, London, S.C.M. Press, and Philadelphia, Pa, Westminster Press, 1945.

The Twentieth Century Encyclopedia of Catholicism

The number of each volume indicates its place in the over-all series and not the order of publication.

TWENTIETH CENTURY ENCYCLOPEDIA OF CATHOLICISM

All titles are subject to change.